KEEPING UP WITH OUR CATHOLIC FAITH

KEEPING UP WITH OUR CATHOLIC FAITH

EXPLAINING CHANGES IN CATHOLIC THINKING SINCE VATICAN II

EDITED BY JACK WINTZ, O.F.M.

Nihil Obstat:
   Rev. John J. Jennings

Imprimi Potest:
   Rev. Roger Huser, O.F.M.
   Provincial

Imprimatur:
   +Joseph L. Bernardin
   Archbishop of Cincinnati
   February 19, 1975

The *Nihil Obstat* and *Imprimatur* are a declaration that a book or pamphlet is considered to be free from doctrinal or moral error. It is not implied that those who have granted the *Nihil Obstat* and *Imprimatur* agree with the contents, opinions, or statements expressed.

Cover design and illustrations by Michael Reynolds

SBN-0-912228-19-9

© 1975 St. Anthony Messenger Press
All rights reserved.
Printed in the U.S.A.

Contents

Introduction vi

Why Stay Catholic?
By Norman Perry, O.F.M. 1

Isn't Anything for Sure Anymore?
By Jack Wintz, O.F.M. 11

Is It Really a Lot Easier to Be Catholic Today?
By John Muthig 23

What's Happening to Conscience?
By Leonard Foley, O.F.M. 37

Isn't Anything a Sin Anymore?
By Leonard Foley, O.F.M. 49

Why Don't They Teach the Ten Commandments Anymore?
By Leonard Foley, O.F.M. 59

Has Confession Gone Out of Style?
By Leonard Foley, O.F.M. 71

Has the Church Lost Our Children?
By Mary Reed Newland 83

Are Catholic Marriage Laws Changing?
By Norman Perry, O.F.M. 93

INTRODUCTION

Many of us Catholics have been passing with difficulty along the path connecting our childhood catechism and current Church teaching. Keeping up with recent developments in the Faith has not been easy or painless for various and complex reasons. Among them, as I see it, are two failings on the part of the Catholic community.

First of all, we who represent the teaching Church have often failed to supply adequate background for the changes which swept over the Catholic landscape since Vatican II. We have not always been sensitive to the needs of our brothers and sisters. We have often not provided satisfying education programs or published enough attractive books and articles, especially on a popular, non-technical level. Nor have we, in an age of shifting viewpoints, demonstrated to our fellow Christian with sufficient care and assurance how traditional values are being preserved.

Introduction

The other failure is the lack of initiative on the part of the learning Church—that is on the part of those who needed to keep informed but who haven't sought out the Catholic teaching that has been available. I refer to those of us who for a variety of reasons stayed aloof from adult education courses or lecture series or from Catholic books, periodicals and diocesan papers that were trying to update us as best they could.

To help both teaching and learning Church alike the *Catholic Update* series was launched by St. Anthony Messenger Press in 1973. These monthly articles sent out in bulk to Catholic parishes represented a new attempt of the teaching Church to explain developments in Catholic Faith and to answer contemporary questions. At the same time, because of its popular (take-the-readers-where-they're-at) style, ordinary Catholics—often bewildered by the changing Church—were provided a tool for enlightening themselves on a wide range of timely topics.

Keeping Up with Our Catholic Faith is the first selection of *Catholic Updates* to be gathered in one volume. This book is an answer to many requests from the U.S. and Canada that the *Update* series be available in unit form. The encouraging feedback and widespread success of *Catholic Update* convince us that the present volume—as well as those to follow—is filling the Christian community's twofold responsibility: to educate and to be educated.

The book also seeks to be an instrument of reconciliation in the Church—a concern highlighted by the Holy Year. Indeed, many of us are sincerely trying to find ways to reconcile the faith of the Apostles and of our childhood catechism with the current teaching of the Church. This book is dedicated to the task of showing the continuity of our enduring Christian values. It hopes to help reconcile the faith of parents with the faith of their children—the faith of the past with that of the present and future. In short, it attempts to bring about peace—that peace which stems from the assurance that the same Christ and the same Spirit have been very much present in our Church from the beginning till now.

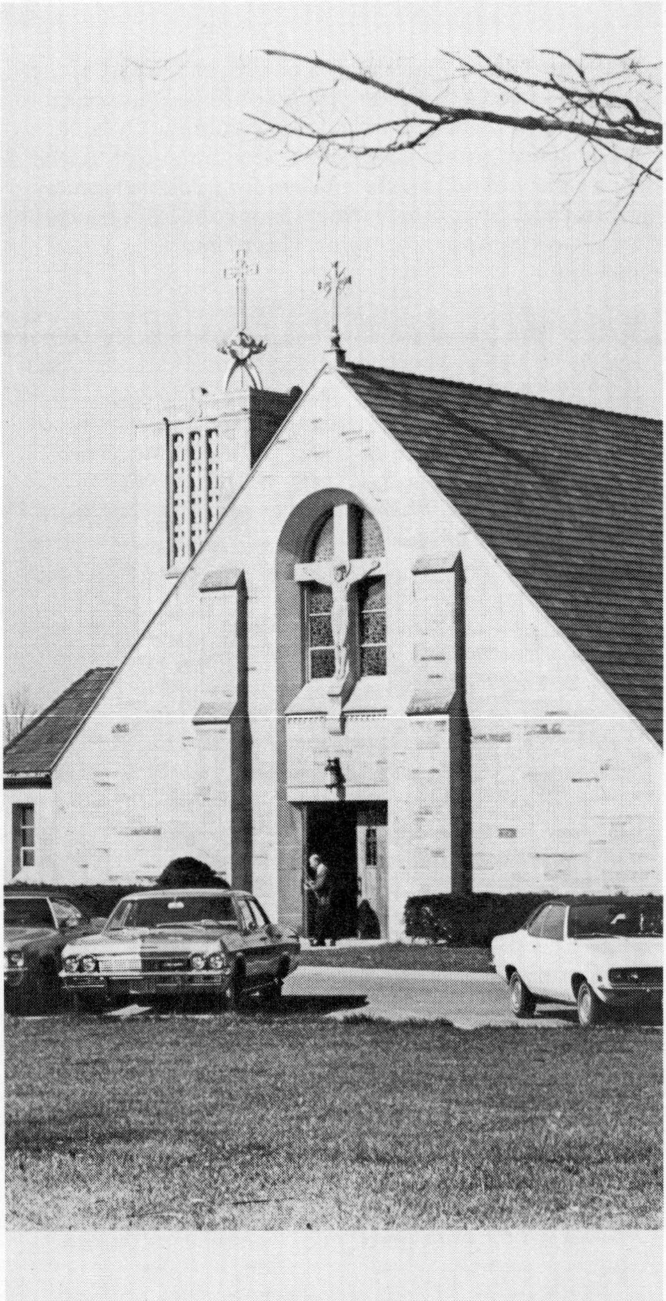

WHY STAY CATHOLIC?

BY NORMAN PERRY, O.F.M.

Everywhere Catholics are disturbed today. Priests leaving the priesthood and marrying, theologians challenging bishops and Vatican congregations, the introduction of rock and folk liturgies, and the suppression of fast and abstinence laws cause many Catholics to wonder if they're still in the same Church. Perhaps you are among them.

Typical of many of us is a fictional Grandma Nicely going to confession. "Bless me, Father, for I have sinned. I'm afraid I'm losing my faith. The Mass doesn't mean anything to me anymore. Since they did away with the Latin it isn't the same everywhere. All the singing and shouting is disturbing. I can't pray. Lent doesn't mean a thing without

Keeping Up with Our Catholic Faith

fasting and abstinence. My daughter is on the pill and says the priest told her it is O.K. Protestants are receiving communion. My father wouldn't recognize the Church today. If you can't believe the Pope, and if one Church is as good as another, *why stay Catholic?*"

Is It Your Question?

Is Grandma Nicely's question your question? Or, if you are undisturbed by change, are you confused about how to answer this question when others ask it? Before going on, stop and ask yourself if you can personally deal with the questions and objections raised above. It's too important for yourself and for others not to deal with them. It's important to ourselves and others that we know why we want to stay Catholic!

The Real Question — What Christ Did and Said

When anyone asks the question "Why be Catholic?" or "Why stay Catholic?" the real issue isn't the sins of priests, changes in unessential customs or the aberrations of individual theologians. The real question, the basic issue, remains: What did Jesus Christ say and do? The real question isn't about folk Masses or fish on Friday. The question is—as always before: Did Christ institute one Church, with an identifiable line of authority and succession, and command it to teach and baptize? Did Christ promise that those who succeeded the apostles as leaders in his Church would be led by the Spirit of truth—his Spirit? Did he say that he would keep the Church from destruction by his own presence? Was it his will that the Church he founded embrace and be embraced by all men? Those packing their suitcases and buying a ticket out of the Church must deal with those questions.

These are the questions of which we must never lose sight. And yet they are the same questions going unasked and unanswered by too many upset Catholics. The things that disturb them are real and they may not be insignificant, but they do not reach the heart of the matter. Failures and abuses do not change or alter the intent of Jesus Christ.

Why Stay Catholic?

Exaggeration of the Facts

Too much attention is given to the voices of dissent. Losses of faith and vocations, though considerable, are still the exception, not the rule. The mass of Catholics still recognize the traditional teaching of the Church and realize what is not in harmony with the creed. While many are bitterly critical of the Pope and bishops, authority remains accepted in the Church. And while some enthusiasts exceed ecumenical limits, most Catholics have actually proceeded more cautiously and reluctantly than others would like.

The Church as One and Apostolic: the Pope and Bishops

To Catholics the Pope remains the successor of St. Peter and the vicar of Christ on earth. He is the symbol of the Church universal. The Pope manifests the Church as one. Should local churches, individual bishops negate the teaching of Christ or stray from it, Catholics continue to recognize the right and duty of the Pope to correct them and restore unity.

Collegiality is not an attempt to sap the authority of the Pope. It seeks, rather, to define more clearly the role of the individual bishops in their dioceses and explain how they act *with* the Pope to maintain the Church as one.

Historians know that there have been constant adjustments in the relationship of Pope and bishops over the centuries. Many times, according to the needs and situations of the era, the Church has moved from centralization to decentralization. In some periods of history most questions were settled on the local or diocesan level while in others nearly all major decisions were referred to the Holy See.

Our age has not been alone in trying to establish the proper weighting of papal and episcopal authority. The problem, of course, is to provide that the rights and office of the Pope are maintained while the voices of the bishops receive due attention. Bishops' conferences have not been usurping authority but exercising responsibility that is theirs as fellow

Keeping Up with Our Catholic Faith

successors of the apostles with the Pope, the successor of Peter.

If at times individual bishops express divergent views or a cardinal criticizes the Pope, modern Catholics should not be scandalized. Until truth has been defined and discerned, it has never been expected that apostles be "yes men." The Scriptures themselves show the presence of disagreement and dissent among various Christian groups. St. Paul challenged St. Peter himself without destroying the Church, Christian unity or the bond of love. Council after council has been called to establish unity in Catholic teaching and doctrine. Never has one single theology, that is, one single theologian's version of the faith, been taught throughout the Church.

That Isn't What the Baltimore Catechism Said

Perhaps American Catholics are unaware of the different schools of theology and the many unsettled theological questions because they were educated with the Baltimore Catechism as their exclusive text. The Baltimore Catechism was a great teaching tool and a great achievement in catechetics. But after some generations of use it becomes evident to educators that the Baltimore Catechism is outdated and has produced some unexpected and undesirable results. Because of the need for brevity, little or no provision was made for showing the historical course of doctrinal development. Only the most common theological positions or theories were taught. The text did not even mention that some answers were by no means certain and that there were other possible explanations or opinions. Because of the question-answer design, there was little or no weighing of the content according to importance. At times we accepted mere opinions of St. Thomas with the same certitude as articles of the creed.

Problems in Our Midst

Should resigning priests and sisters, marrying bishops, too-sumptuous convents and bishops' homes really shake our

Why Stay Catholic?

faith? Hardly! First of all, we cannot know the reasons behind personal decisions, much less judge others as sinners. And even if we could, we know that the Church is made up of sinners as well as saints. It was Christ who founded it so and compared it to a wheat field full of weeds. Aware of our own failures, we shouldn't be surprised at evil in others— be they popes, bishops, priests, sisters or anyone else. The lives of St. Francis of Assisi and Catherine of Siena remind us that the Church has always had to urge her members to penance and reform.

Let's put aside our supercritical pose for a while and look at the good in the Church. Thousands of missionary priests, brothers and sisters, binding the wounds of lepers and caring for orphans in foreign lands, manifest holiness in the Church. Millions of good Catholic mothers and fathers striving to lead decent lives and sacrificing for their children are evidence of goodness. God does reach people through the Church and sacraments.

That some even abandon the faith altogether shouldn't dismay us. Christ himself witnessed desertion on the day he promised the Eucharist. In the wake of too-little-loving and too-little-believing listeners, Christ asked the disciples if they too would leave him. Peter answered for all men of faith, "Lord, to whom shall we go? You have the words of eternal life."

What Price Uniformity?

No doubt travelers abroad are disappointed and unfulfilled by Masses celebrated in Spanish, French or Italian. Surely it would be inspiring to them to find Mass said in the same way and same language as at home. No doubt in earlier times the omnipresence of the Latin liturgy strengthened our sense of unity with Catholics everywhere. But what price uniformity? How many Catholics travel abroad? Shouldn't our first consideration be the millions of people attending Mass in their own parish churches? Surely it is of far greater importance that they understand the word of God proclaimed to them in their own language.

Keeping Up with Our Catholic Faith

And if young people are better able to pray and express their worship in a style of music that means little to older people, why can't each generation use what best inspires them to pray? Why not a more solemn liturgy for older folks at 9 o'clock and a folk Mass with guitars for the kids at 10 o'clock? Both are fine so long as the music in each style has artistic value and suits the liturgical parts of the Mass. The fact is that the Church does retain the bond of union. The faith is still one in Jesus Christ. That fact is confused or obscured by too much emphasis on unessential differences rather than the essentials of faith and practices that unite us.

That the Mass is today more frequently offered in different languages and surrounded by varying customs and ceremonies doesn't change a reality that has been long present. From apostolic times the Mass and sacraments have been offered and administered in different tongues with different ceremonies. The Church has long known a multiplicity of rites. While our grandparents used Latin for their liturgical ceremonies, Greeks worshiped in Greek, Russians in Russian. No one called that disunity. We were all offering the sacrifice of Jesus, reapeating the acts and words of Jesus at the Last Supper, and above all, thanking and praising the Father as Jesus did.

Today we profess the same faith—no matter what language we use to proclaim the creed. We are baptized with the baptism of Christ. It is the same word and revelation of Jesus that is preached and accepted in any Catholic church. It is the same Christ who is our Lord. We are united in the same Bishop of Rome. There is the unity, the oneness, that marks the Catholic Church and Christ's Church.

The Important Things Haven't Changed

The important things haven't changed. The Gospel is the Gospel proclaimed by Christ. The Church hasn't changed it, though at times we have come to better understand it.

The Mass, the sacraments, the creed, all link us with the past. They are the precious heritage we have received from our fathers in the faith. Accidentals and incidentals have

Why Stay Catholic?

changed from the beginning. While the apostles were still living, the Church abandoned the dietary laws of the Jews. Church buildings weren't built until the third or fourth century. Religious orders appeared on the scene only after two or three centuries. The way of the cross and the rosary were prayer forms introduced late in the life of the Church— 1,200 years after Christ. Benediction of the Blessed Sacrament first appears in the 16th century. A new code of disciplinary law—The Code of Canon Law—was published as late as 1917.

Does it mean, then, that the Church is really no longer the same if some Catholics aren't very enthusiastic about praying the rosary or the bishops decide that Friday abstinence has served its usefulness and ought to be a law no longer?

St. Paul might not recognize everything in the Church today. But he would know the Catholic Church for the Church of Christ. He would discover the Gospel, the celebration of the Eucharist, and the sacraments. He would find the successors of the apostles in the bishops and the successor of St. Peter in the Bishop of Rome. And those are the same things we discern. Historians, newspaper editors, the man on the street have no difficulty tracing the course of the Catholic Church throughout the centuries and identifying the Church of today as the Church of St. Augustine and St. Francis. The characteristics, the identifying marks are the same.

> "Catholicism is presently undergoing a crisis. But this is nothing new. It has survived crises before and will survive them again. Schools of thought (and theology) will come and go, but Catholics believe that the Church will remain—and so far it has. As long as there are Catholics who really do love one another, Catholicism remains both believable and catholic."
>
> *Ken Eberhard, St. Anthony Messenger.*

Keeping Up with Our Catholic Faith

Questions for Discussion

1. Why is it important to ourselves and others that we know why we want to stay Catholic? Is being able to put into words *why* they believe more important today for parents than it was for our grandparents?

2. What does the author say lies at the heart of Jesus' teaching about the Church?

3. What are some of the benefits the Church can gain by allowing divergent views regarding Church laws and decrees? What are some of the essential truths in the Church which have remained unchanged throughout history?

4. Many people are upset over the divisions which the changes in the Church have brought about. How do we reconcile Jesus giving us his peace and saying the following: "Do you think I have come to establish peace on this earth? I assure you, the contrary is true; I have come for division."

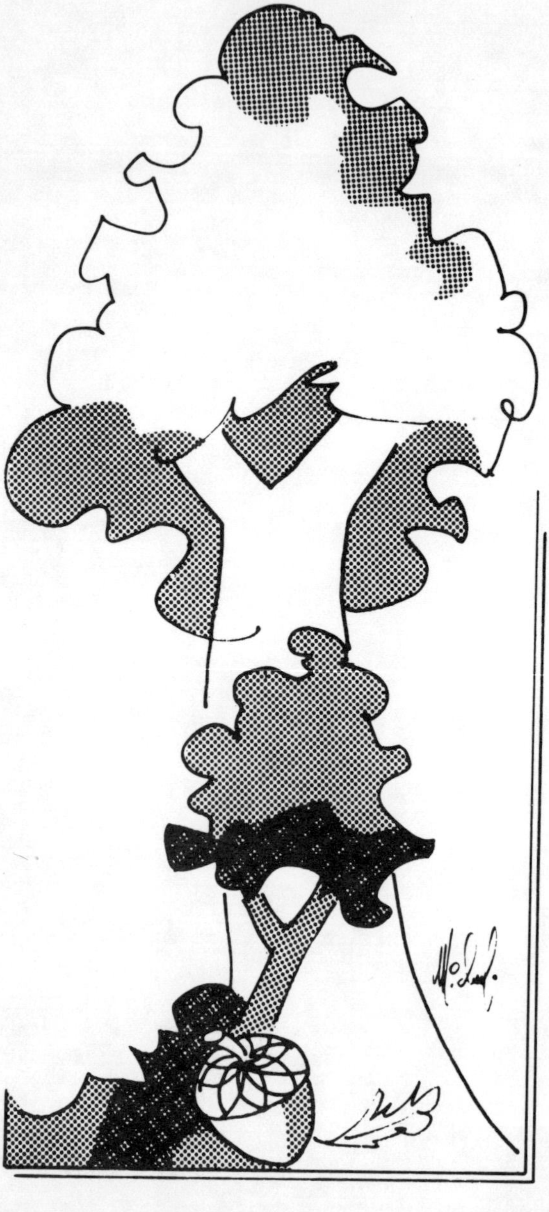

ISN'T ANYTHING FOR SURE ANYMORE?

BY JACK WINTZ, O.F.M.

When my grandfather was 12, he used to jump from a lower limb of his backyard oak tree. He tried it again when he was 25 and sprained an ankle. He took the leap one more time when he was 68 and broke both legs.

"Isn't anything for sure anymore?" he moaned as they slid him into the ambulance.

Well, one thing that's sure, they could have told him, is that the tree is much taller now than when he was 12 and, as for his bones, they're more brittle now, too. It was the same oak tree—that's for sure—but trees have a way of growing and changing, and he should have taken that change into consideration.

Keeping Up with Our Catholic Faith

In a similar way, you and I may feel discomforted, if not crippled, by a changing Church, which is growing as relentlessly as any oak. No matter how desperately we cling to a past image of the Church and insist that it doesn't change, it seems that the Church itself just grows blissfully on. "For, as the centuries succeed one another," acknowledges Vatican II's *Constitution on Divine Revelation,* "the Church constantly moves forward towards the fullness of divine truth until the words of God reach their complete fulfillment in her."

Jesus tried to warn you and me about this. He said his Kingdom was like the tiny mustard seed which grows into a tree big enough to hold lots of birds. He compared it to a man who planted a tree and then forgot about it. But his forgetting and ignoring it did not stop it from growing. Time and again he used seed and growth images to describe his Kingdom. He warned us against putting new wine in old wineskins. And knowing life to be a continuous struggle between defenders of the past and advocates of the future, he praised the flexibility of the guy who could take from his storeroom things both new and old.

What Is for Sure—the Super-truths

The most fundamental things in Christianity's storeroom— the "super-truths" that really count—have not changed. These things are for sure: a loving God made us after his own image and likeness...He sent his Son to be our brother and he is at work in us now through his Spirit... Jesus saves us...He is present in the Eucharist...He is present in his body, the community of Christians, his Church...He is the core and cornerstone of all reality and history...The universe is basically good and with Christ the good will eventually triumph over evil. Love will triumph over hatred...
Man is free...God is forgiving and heals our lives, no matter how we've messed them up...By dying with Christ to selfishness we rise to a richer life...By being prayerful, humble, loving toward God and neighbor and open to the touch of Christ's saving body, we find meaning, happiness and redemption.

Isn't Anything for Sure Anymore?

All these values and more, integrated in the living reality of Christ, form the enduring bedrock of our faith and provide us with the security and foothold we need in changing times.

Stop Moving the Targets

Yet you and I do not always feel this security, and we are disturbed by the many changes of our age. We cry desperately for stability and sameness. We grasp at times, like drowning men, for the solid planks and clear-cut formulas of our grade school catechism, but they have drifted downstream ahead of us. We feel a lack of firm guidance from those in authority. We feel as aimless as arrows sailing at moving targets. The cool eternity of Gregorian chant has been replaced by twanging guitars, the changeless Latin by varying vernaculars. Ironclad dogmas and rigid ethics have been exchanged for flexible, form-fitting doctrinal quickies and moral stretchies. We yearn for the stone columns of orthodoxy and an iron line of command where Pete Parish backs the priest, the priest backs the prelate, and the prelate, the Pope. If the Pope, once and for all, just declared infallibly "what's going on," we would feel much more secure.

From Safety Vault to Living Spirit

The catechisms and the dogma texts of the first half of this century presented us with an immovable system of doctrine. And our faith was largely an intellectual faith in *contents*, in lists of firm formulas and precise answers, rather than a faith of total surrender to the person of Christ. These contents were like so many solid bars of truths and stacks of exact definitions stored safely away in the safety vault of the Church. If a question arose or a doubt sprang up, we serenely went to the safety vault and were relieved to see everything in order. This gave us a sense of security but left us unprepared for the growth and insight explosion surrounding Vatican II.

God guides the Church to the truth not so much by putting a freeze on the printed page or on a doctrinal system but by keeping his living Spirit with the Church. More than a cen-

Keeping Up with Our Catholic Faith

tury ago Cardinal John Henry Newman wrote his famous *Essay on the Development of Christian Doctrine*. He noted that doctrines develop because they are basically ideas, and ideas exist in living people, not in books. As people change and grow in knowledge, naturally their ideas change and develop. If the same development goes on in the living Church we can see why today's theologians often stress that faith demands not so much a blind clinging to the mind-set of a previous era as an ongoing faith and reliance on Christ's living Spirit ever discerning the changing contours of the current scene.

Vatican II itself stated that the "tradition which comes from the apostles develops in the Church with the help of the Holy Spirit. For there is a growth in the understanding of the realities and the words which have been handed down."

Although the contents of our faith are important, it is Jesus' living person—as revealed by the whole "happening" of his life, death and resurrection—that is the source of revelation. He said, "He who has seen *me* has seen the Father" and "*I* am the way, the truth and the life." The real source of our faith is not merely a set of doctrines but rather the person of Christ still living and "happening" in the Church today. When he left his apostles, Jesus assured them of his living presence: "When the Spirit of truth comes, he will lead you to the complete truth."

From Acorn to Oak

Like a tree, the Church grows and develops. The tiny acorn grows into the mature oak, and yet it always keeps its identity as an oak. So also the Church can grow and develop and still keep its same identity.

Fifty years ago, almost all Catholics from the Pope on down thought that evolution was contradictory to the Bible and a threat to Catholic doctrine. But human knowledge progressed, our worldview developed, the Bible became more fully understood, and now most Catholics can take the possibility of evolution in easy stride. Vatican II can calmly note that "the

Isn't Anything for Sure Anymore?

human race has passed from a rather static concept of reality to a more dynamic, evolutionary one."

The Church has evolved in many ways. For example, St. Peter, the first head of the Church, once wrote that slaves should be submissive to their masters even if unfairly treated (1 Pet. 2, 18). In the worldview of his time, slavery was an accepted part of the social system. But Jesus had planted the seed-idea of human dignity, freedom, equality, and it has been developing over the centuries, so that now the Church sees any slavery system as anti-Christian and unacceptable.

On one level the Church is a human institution and it must struggle for the truth in pain and insecurity, much like any other institution. In guarding its past values, it can be overly cautious or defensive just like you and me, the human beings of which it is composed. It may feel threatened at first by the teachings of a Galileo or Copernicus, a Darwin or a Freud, but sooner or later it will incorporate their valid contributions into its own doctrine.

Stop the Worldviews, I Want Some Rest!

As one worldview changes and gives place to another, our approach to truth changes. A primitive worldview, for example, once pictured God directly operating the universe. He sat on a mountaintop or cloud and personally hurled the lightning bolts and rolled out the thunder. Wind and rain were under his fingertip supervision. A primitive man's notion of divine providence could be so tied up with his worldview that if you or I told him the lightning was governed by scientific laws, he might slug us with his stone hatchet, for in his eyes we would appear to be denying divine providence. We know better than this. We know that divine providence can be just as much at work in a worldview which sees God using scientific laws to control the universe.

In each age it is hard for us to sort out and distinguish between our faith and the culturally colored lenses through which we view that faith.

Keeping Up with Our Catholic Faith

The Baltimore Catechism was basically founded on the worldview of 1884, the year it was first written, during the closing days of the Third Plenary Council of Baltimore. Though revisions were eventually made, the worldview of 1884 was the basic framework of the catechism still taught in the 1950's. Such a viewpoint was prior to the automobile and air travel, radio and television, modern psychology and the computer, not to mention the dune buggy and the disposable diaper. Surely these developments, even the trivial ones, have tempered and shaped our way of looking at truth. No wonder that the worldview smuggled in with our catechism needs some adjusting.

Our worldview is always changing. And according to Alvin Toffler in his fascinating book *Future Shock,* these worldviews are changing faster and faster so that man needs an ever-increasing ability to cope with change. Vatican II already noted in *The Church in the Modern World* that "history itself speeds along on so rapid a course that an individual can scarcely keep abreast of it" and that the "scientific spirit exerts a new kind of impact on the cultural sphere and on modes of thought. Technology is now transforming the face of the earth."

In the worldview of the Baltimore Catechism an accent was placed on the gulf between the natural and the supernatural, the secular and the divine. Recently a worldview has been emerging which sees a blending of the divine with the secular—a blending perhaps best symbolized by God's stepping into human (secular) clothing at the Incarnation. Those holding to the former worldview which stresses the separation between the secular and the divine are much more disturbed by priests in politics and by nuns in civilian dress than those holding to the latter.

The clash of worldviews within the Church does not necessarily mean a failure of the Holy Spirit. More and more man is realizing that it is precisely through conflict that truth emerges. Disagreement spawns the advance of knowledge and helps further growth. As Rosemary Haughton says in

Isn't Anything for Sure Anymore?

The Changing Church, "It is by conflict that truth and error become distinguishable and truth takes one more step forward."

Pew Power

Not too many centuries or even decades ago, priests, for the most part, were the only formally educated members of the Church. The ordinary man in the pews, not having had the opportunity of formal schooling, looked up to the priest as the man with all the answers. The priest, in turn, was thought to be in touch with an immovable system of defined truth. Many people apparently based their security on the priest and on the allegedly changeless framework of doctrine which gave him solid backing.

Now, however, the worldview has changed. The man in the pew, conceivably at least, can be as well informed as the priest. And truth is no longer viewed as a superstructure of fixed definitions. Because there is more power in the pews and because truth is seen as developing rather than static, more and more priests and sisters are hesitant to issue pat answers to questions. This apparent hesitancy on the part of priests and sisters disturbs many of us because it conflicts with the role we had expected them to play.

A recent survey by *St. Anthony Messenger* magazine revealed a rather extensive sense of irritation in people about this. There were many complaints about priests being evasive and indecisive, sisters and religion teachers giving questioners the runaround, confessors hedging and compromising and being inconsistent. In many cases, no doubt, they do this to a fault. But from another standpoint they are merely reflecting the above-mentioned worldview. They sometimes see their role as that of guiding people to form their own decisions and to rely more on their own responsibility. They want to share what enlightenment they have with others, give direction and principles so that the others can form their own consciences and listen to the Spirit within them. But sometimes they don't feel they can always give an absolute or ready-made answer to questions. On the one hand they want to lead others to development and maturity, while

Keeping Up with Our Catholic Faith

on the other they are fearful of keeping someone a child by assuming his responsibility.

The Truth Will Triumph

Our greatest sense of security comes from Christ's promise that he would be with his Church until the end of time. The Good News of the Gospel will prevail and triumph because Jesus' Spirit guides the Church infallibly to the fullness of truth. He speaks through the community of the faithful as a whole, especially through his teaching ministers and through the head of that community, the Pope, but also through the grass roots.

Our belief in Christ's Spirit guiding us lovingly and infallibly, if a bit unpredictably, is one of those consoling and "for sure" things we all seem to need these days. Yet, just how Christ guides us infallibly is not perfectly clear. An important part of this unerring guidance is papal infallibility, but this notion has always been surrounded by some misconceptions.

Many Catholics, in fact, seem to have founded too much of their security on a misunderstood notion of papal infallibility— as if the Holy Father can instantly clear up any confusing issue by dashing off an infallible decree. The Pope, though specially guided by the Holy Spirit, remains a limited human being struggling for the truth amid changing worldviews. The use of papal infallibility is extremely limited and does not apply to encyclicals, as the Baltimore Catechism itself clearly stated: "The Pope can teach without speaking infallibly; for example, he does this in his encyclical letters." Only two clear cases of papal infallibility have been witnessed over the last 100 years—pronouncements on the Immaculate Conception and the Assumption of Our Lady.

Infallibility, therefore, is neither an instant cure for confusion nor a handy tool for making new declarations of truth. Rather it helps discern or declare what is *already held to* by the Church as a whole. "Ideally," writes Father Melvin L. Farrell, S.S., "the Pope should simply declare, or make explicit, what the Holy Spirit has been bringing to consciousness in the People of God as a whole. In other words, revealed truth rises from the faith experience of the Church as a whole, not from the Pope alone."

The same view is attributed to theologian Karl Rahner by Monika Hellwig in her book *What Are the Theologians Saying?* Presenting Rahner's position, she writes that the Holy Father can claim infallibility only "where it is clear that he is giving expression to the faith of the whole Church, that is, when he is speaking for the whole assembly of the faithful." According to Rahner, Hellwig continued, Pope Paul did not claim infallibility in his encyclical *Humanae Vitae* "but simply gave his personal judgment. He could not have claimed infallibility because his commission, which had studied the tradition from the past and the evidence from the world community of the faithful in the present, had advised him to the contrary of his own judgment."

Some theologians would argue with Hellwig's strong-sounding statement by insisting that the Pope has a prophetic role—and is not merely a consensus gatherer. And what good is the prophetic office of the Church if the Pope can not stand "over and against" a majority opinion of a commission? The whole question needs further study and dialogue.

Isn't Anything for Sure Anymore?

Zeroing in on the issue of papal infallibility is perhaps not so crucial in answering our question as is concentrating on the broader infallibility of the Holy Spirit guiding the whole interacting Church—Pope, hierarchy, laity—to the complete truth. "Know that I am with you always; yes, to the end of time." This promise of Jesus to the seedling Apostolic Church indicates that the core reality of the Church will always remain, namely, the living person of Christ himself. The seedling has grown and will continue to grow and develop, but Christ, along with the values he reveals and embodies, will remain amid all the change.

Keeping Up with Our Catholic Faith

The Christian, it seems, lives neither entirely in the past nor entirely in the future but on the cutting edge of the present. He stands on the edge of constant change, but "beneath all the changes," Vatican II assures us in *The Church in the Modern World*, "there are many realities which do not change and which have their ultimate foundation in Christ, who is the same yesterday and today, yes, and forever."

Questions for Discussion

1. Why is it that some people like variety and thrive on change, but others become unhappy and insecure because of changes?

2. Cardinal Newman, almost 100 years ago said, "In a higher world it is otherwise; but here below to live is to change, and to be perfect is to have changed often." Do you agree with him? Why or why not?

3. Do you accept the author's assessment that a "clash of worldviews within the Church does not necessarily mean a failure of the Holy Spirit"? What examples can you think of to support your view?

4. What are some of the different ways we can define or view the Church? What definitions or views of the Church were stressed before Vatican II? What now?

5. The author states that infallibility is neither an instant cure for confusion nor a handy tool for making new declarations of truth. Rather it helps discern or declare what is *already held to* by the Church as a whole. Why is the notion of papal infallibility often misunderstood?

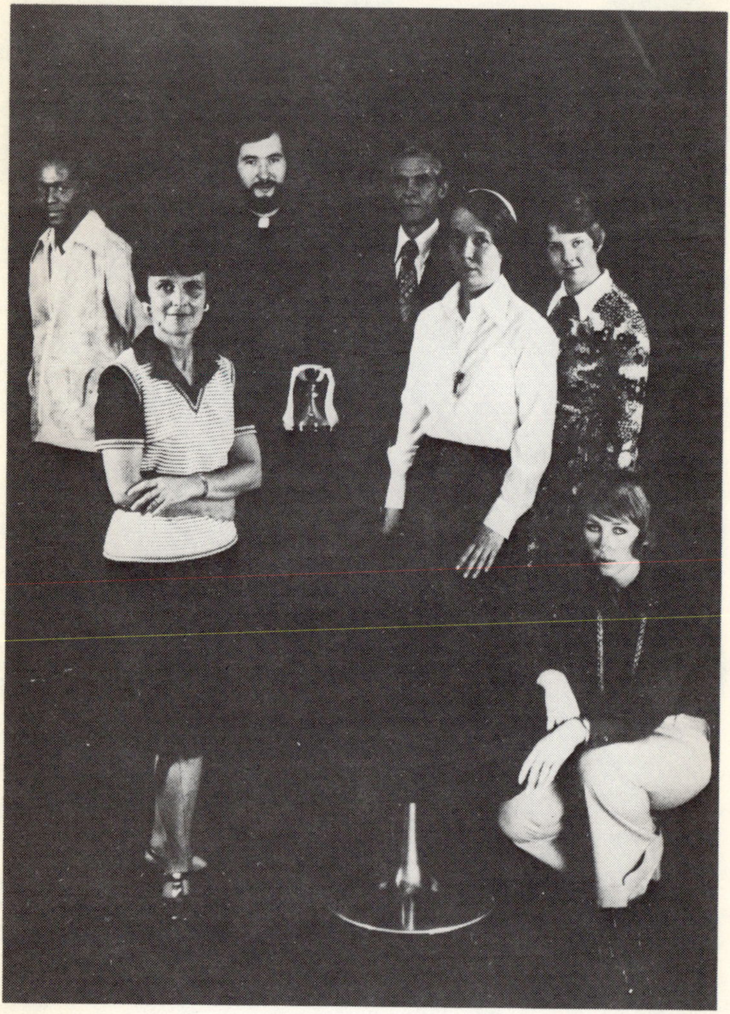

IS IT REALLY A LOT EASIER TO BE CATHOLIC TODAY?

BY JOHN MUTHIG

The appealing aromas from my mother's kitchen on Fridays at about 5 p.m. would have kept Christopher Columbus from setting sail for the New World. The "no meat" day at our house meant extra-special eating. We could always count on mom to whip up one of her famous meatless Italian dishes or to buy fresh lobster, crab or bluefish at the market. Even then, Friday abstinence wasn't hard for our family.

In response to a man-in-the-street question asked by a Catholic newspaper, the majority of Catholics interviewed said that they felt it was a lot easier to be Catholic today than when they were kids. "After our strict upbringing,"

Keeping Up with Our Catholic Faith

answered one man, "the Church has gone permissive. You don't have to fast anymore, you can eat meat on Friday. The Catholic religion is getting watered-down!"

Some mentioned the fast and abstinence law change as a symptom of weakening in Church discipline. It *is* a lot easier to be Catholic today, they said. The Church seems to be losing its commitment to penance and to carrying the cross. Others noted a breakdown in the dedication of Sisters to their vocations and a general decline in interest among the laity in traditional Catholic organizations or in special religious devotions and services.

If you took a poll of Catholics in your parish, the results would probably show that very few still abstain from meat on Friday, that the enrollment in the Holy Name Society has been slipping for the last few years and that special novenas and Benediction services have been drastically reduced, if not cut completely.

Sounds depressing. But it's only a partial picture. Actually, if you scratch below the surface, you'll find that the Church is officially asking much more of Catholics today than in the past, and that, by and large, Catholics are putting out much more. For Catholics who really understand their Church, being a Catholic today is as hard as or even harder than it ever was!

WHAT WAS WRONG WITH NOT EATING MEAT?

The Baltimore Catechism explained that the Church commanded us to abstain "in order that we might control the desires of the flesh, raise our minds and hearts more freely to God, and make satisfaction for sin."

At our house, at least, Friday meant parole from the week's fare of beef and potatoes. Sure, once in a while "no meat" was an inconvenience; but as for controlling the desires of the flesh, praying more easily or doing penance for sin . . . well, we didn't accomplish any of these things by eating mother's meatless masterpieces.

Is It Really a Lot Easier to Be Catholic Today?

And our family was not alone. "Changing circumstances have made some of our people feel that renunciation of the eating of meat is not always and for everyone the most effective means of practicing penance," wrote the American bishops when they changed the fast and abstinence laws in 1966. "Meat was once an exceptional form of food; now it is commonplace."

For a poor family in the Depression years, giving up the rare treat of a really good piece of meat and eating instead a tuna casserole made up of 99 percent noodles was penance — giving until it hurts.

But tuna noodle casseroles have improved a great deal since the Depression. So, by 1966, the American bishops knew that the time had come to translate the unchanging obligation to do penance into concrete terms that a nation with a Gross National Product of $750,000,000,000 (in 1966) could relate to.

First they turned to tradition. What were the three time-honored ways of making reparation for sin? Fasting, prayer and works of mercy. These three practices, then, became the foundation for new rules for American Catholics on doing penance.

WHAT NEW RULES FOR PENANCE?

Okay, they aren't rules, really. Just very serious suggestions from our Church's leaders on ways to do penance today. The bishops took away most of the obligations to fast and abstain, as everyone knows. But in the same breath they awarded first place among all the possible ways of doing penance to voluntary fasting and abstaining. What's more, they suggested new twists to brighten up these traditional practices.

Americans spend about $11 billion annually on alcohol. So the bishops hinted that, if giving up meat on Friday wasn't really "giving until it hurts," abstaining

Keeping Up with Our Catholic Faith

from beer or martinis on that day might sting a little harder.

Chances are good, though, that you never heard about this suggestion. When the changes were made in 1966, the news media grabbed on to only part of the bishops' message — that it wasn't a sin anymore to eat meat on Fridays, etc. Now if the bishops had been writing those headlines, they would have keyed in on something else. Over your morning coffee you might have read:

SELF-DENIAL STRESSED FOR CATHOLICS

BISHOPS PUT PIZZAZ IN PENANCE

Some Catholics did get the message, though, and applied their own creativity to the practice of fasting by agreeing to live on a welfare food budget during Lent. In November, 1972, the Priests' Senate of the Archdiocese of Detroit prompted Cardinal John Dearden to ask Catholics in his diocese to fast and abstain on Election Day to ask God's help in voting.

Stress on prayer as a form of penance was brought into play especially over the question of observing Advent. With Christmas office parties, holiday gatherings, Yuletide carols and festive decorations all around, how could the

Is It Really a Lot Easier to Be Catholic Today?

Catholic keep a spirit of penance during December? The bishops suggested focusing on the liturgy. Make a point of meditating on the Advent liturgical texts, they said, and couple this with family and community religious observances. Then the season will come into its own again.

Then works of mercy. The Bishops of Vatican II wanted penitential practice in the renewed Church to be external and social as well as internal and individual. So the American bishops applied that principle to Friday as a special day of penance for sin. "It would bring great glory to God and good to souls," they wrote, "if Fridays found our people
    l) doing volunteer work in hospitals
    2) visiting the sick
    3) serving the needs of the aged and the lonely
    4) instructing the young in the faith
    5) participating as Christians in community affairs
    6) and meeting our obligations to our families, our friends, our neighbors and our community, including our parishes, with special zeal . . . ."

Check over that list again. Can you find anything there that sounds easier than not eating meat on Friday?

Remember how you used to cut out the fast and abstinence laws from the diocesan paper and tape them to the kitchen bulletin board or the front of the refrigerator? Well, why not clip this list of works of mercy and put it where you'll be sure to see it on Friday as a reminder to commemorate in a special way the day Christ died.

BUT IT'S NOT WORKING!

The big problem today is not that the Church is making it easier for Catholics to practice their faith, but that it is a lot easier for Catholics to say "no" to the Church's suggestions. The Church could and did command us to abstain on Fridays. But so many of the hard things the Church asks of us today require a free response. You

Keeping Up with Our Catholic Faith

can't very easily command that a person sharpen his attention during the lessons at Masses in Advent or that he visit the sick on Fridays.

Now years of strictly following laws have left some of us stiff-jointed when it comes to making free responses. Yet if something is really important to us or is truly central to the way we live, that something won't vanish in a puff of smoke as soon as the laws which used to envelop it are dropped.

We left Christopher Columbus at my mother's kitchen. Actually he would have felt more comfortable with my grandmother. She, too, was born in Genoa and would have been brimming over with pride to have "Colombo" as a dinner guest.

At our house, though, the explorer would have been just another mouth to feed. Like most other Americans, we "celebrated" Columbus Day only as long as businesses and schools closed down. Now most schools and shops stay open, and most Americans no longer mark the holiday.

If schools and offices stayed open on Christmas, however, we would still celebrate the holiday in our homes as best we could even though the *legal* celebration of the day no longer existed. Christmas is a vital part of our lives as Americans and as Christians, whereas Columbus Day means little to most of us.

The *legal* aspects of penance — the laws which once bound us under pain of sin to fast and abstain — are gone. But if we really understand the Christian's serious responsibility to do penance and repent, we'll continue to deny ourselves even though the laws on penance have become suggestions. If you're rusty on the obligation to do penance, these Bible passages may be helpful to you:

Mt. 16:21-28. This passage contains the familiar

Is It Really a Lot Easier to Be Catholic Today?

words, "If a man wishes to come after me he must deny his very self, take up his cross and follow in my footsteps."

Mt. 25:31-46. The scene is the Last Judgment. The virtuous ask Jesus: "When did we see you hungry and feed you ... sick or in prison and go to see you?" "In so far as you did this to one of the least of these brothers of mine you did it to me," answers Jesus.

Is. 58. On fast days the Jews were cutting down on food but not on anything else. Isaiah scolds them for mistreating their workers, carousing around and having fist fights on days of penance. Then he lays on the line what it means to keep a fast. His suggestions closely parallel the works of mercy in Mt. 25:31-46 and also the American bishops' 1966 statement.

THOSE NEW NUNS!

But changes in the fast laws are not the only examples which some Catholics give of the new Church permissiveness. Many Catholics, especially the products of parochial schools, are troubled by the changes in religious orders of women. They recall how they admired the nuns for their dedication to poverty, chastity and obedience and for their austere life-style.

But look at today's nuns! You are likely to find Sisters, dressed in contemporary fashion, employed by a state-run poverty program that officially has nothing to do with spreading religion. Their dedication seems to be wearing thin, their commitment to humanism seems stronger than their commitment to Jesus.

I think back to a cousin of mine who used to visit our family — but only on special occasions. We children were fascinated how she survived 90 degree heat in her black religious habit with her face boxed in by the tightly fitting headpiece.

Keeping Up with Our Catholic Faith

Now we see our cousin more often; her order believes that it is good for her to be closer to her family, and she is always an inspiration to us when she visits. Her new mobility has also given her the freedom to continue her education in summer school and to help out in a parish religious education project in her spare time.

My cousin is more comfortable in her simple suit, which doesn't violate her vow of poverty, and short veil and medallion which clearly identify her as a religious. Others in her order have given up wearing the habit. While my cousin feels that there is something to be said for letting her clothes be a sign of her inward dedication, she is the first to insist that we shouldn't judge the dedication of others by what they wear on their backs.

Several Sisters from her order have opened up a storefront center in the inner-city. They were the first to admit that their limited resources and small staff could do little in the face of the problems they are confronting among the city poor.

But theirs was social work with a difference. Governments, they noted, do social work for some*thing*. The Sisters are working for some*one*. Concern for the individual as an important creation of God and as a man redeemed by Jesus spark operations at their center.

One Sister from the center was planning to live at a house of prayer for a year to make sure that she was not losing sight of the spiritual dimension of her work. At the house of prayer she will leave all social work behind and engage only in deepening her relationship with Jesus.

Perhaps no group in the post-Vatican II Church has done more than the Sisters in tailoring the Christian traditions of prayer, poverty and service to the 20th century scene. If we just look at the externals, we may have our doubts about this, but usually these doubts go up in smoke after more careful study.

Is It Really a Lot Easier to Be Catholic Today?

"You are free," wrote French theologian Yves Congar, "not only to pray how you like, sing your spiritual songs to your own tune, but also to undertake some spiritual work or other. If you want to you can found a new religious congregation . . . I am not joking! There is no end to the originality of the saints."

Creative freedom, like that spoken of by Father Congar, is permitting today's Sisters to reach the fullness of their potential for Christian service. And, for sure, along with this potential for originality and creative freedom in the Church comes the risk of shipwreck. The Sisters in the inner-city center are boiling over with enthusiasm and good works today, but what about tomorrow? There is a chance they could lose the real Spirit behind their work; they could put down the cross.

But just because you may wind up shipwrecked doesn't mean you should stay in dry dock. The purpose of a ship is to sail. Sisters, like lay people, have been given more freedom to chart their own course. In many cases the voyage has become more rigorous than ever before.

THE CHRISTIAN GROWS UP

Religious people must inch their way toward their full potential in the faith just as children must mature bit by bit toward adulthood. To grow we need both rules and freedoms. Too much of either can be toxic.

"If religion is your God, then it may be that God is not fully your religion," wrote Father Thomas G. Savage, S.J. What he meant by "religion" was ritual and practices that go along with faith. Too many rules or rules obeyed just out of habit can mask the "why" behind some practices — like fasting and abstaining.

Then, too, the Christian with too much freedom is like a runner with too many feet or a knitter with too much yarn. Instead of running faster, the athelete trips over his own feet; instead of getting more scarves made,

Keeping Up with Our Catholic Faith

the knitter spends a lot more time unravelling knots.

But rules followed intelligently or self-imposed are fuel for getting us where we want to go spiritually. Family members who choose to eat on a welfare budget during Lent "curb the desires of the flesh," as we used to say, and share the lot of the poor who are always hungry. The executive who voluntarily translates the old command to abstain from meat into a self-imposed obligation to stay off whiskey sours on Fridays spotlights in his life the things that are indispensable and underplays what doesn't matter.

Freedom when respected for what it can do unleashes our creative potential at full blast. Often without really making the connection, Catholics are living out the 1966 statement of the American bishops on penance. These new penances are almost always more time-consuming and more tiring than abstaining from meat or fasting ever was.

POWER TO THE PEOPLE

The Pope is pleased. That's how I would interpret the Holy Father's decision to abolish minor orders, formerly preliminary steps to priestly ordination, and the major order of subdiaconate. These offices are obsolete, said the Pope, since lay people have taken over many of the roles once assigned to these men.

Lay men and women, knowing that lectoring or serving as leaders of song or parish liturgical planners cuts into leisure time and means more work, are often excited and thrilled to give more.

The diaconate is now open to lay men in several American dioceses. No special salary or extraordinary honors come with ordination to the diaconate; only the chance to serve more completely. Candidates for the diaconate attend seminary classes, usually for two years, on Saturdays or weeknights. Their reward is in giving.

Is It Really a Lot Easier to Be Catholic Today?

Have you ever attended a meeting of your parish council or parochial school board or liturgy committee? If you have, then you know what giving until it hurts is all about.

The 1966 call to penance by the American bishops wasn't just a paper tiger for many Catholics. What about you? Your parish doesn't have a parish council or you don't know the first thing about working on a school board or in the PTA? Well, perhaps your community has an organization called FISH, an ecumenical group which helps your neighbors in many ways — providing rides for the sick and the elderly, offering a willing ear to someone who needs to talk, volunteering tutoring services, etc.

Creative Catholics are needed by community organizations like the Heart Fund, Big Brothers, free clinics, the cancer society, Girl and Boy Scouts and Birthright. The message of the American bishops is simple: Be aware of your possibilities as well as your obligations to do penance.

Some Catholics still feel that it is a lot easier to be Catholic today. Their spiritual life could probably use a tune up. Perhaps you are one of them. Your parish or local Catholic high school may be sponsoring a worthwhile adult religious education program. Try stopping by the nearest Catholic bookstore. The clerk can recommend some new titles that might help you.

Rules are fewer; obligations are the same; ways we can meet our Christian obligations have doubled and trebled. Now Catholics have the freedom to say "no." But Catholics who understand that the freedom of the sons of God is not a lifelong vacation with pay will find themselves saying "yes" much more than before.

Keeping Up with Our Catholic Faith

Questions for Discussion

1. According to the author some Catholics feel the change in the fast and abstinence law is a good example of a general weakening in Church discipline. Do you agree? What examples can you cite either for or against your position?

2. This chapter quotes six methods suggested by the American Bishops to make Friday a special day of penance for sin. Is it easier to observe the Friday abstinence law or to follow the six suggestions?

3. Try to make a list of concrete acts of penance that would be realistic for Americans today.

4. The author says, "The big problem today is not that the Church is making it easier for Catholics to practice their faith, but that it is a lot easier for Catholics to say 'no' to the Church's suggestions." Do you think that is true? If so, why?

5. In this chapter the author interprets the Holy Father's decision to abolish minor orders and the major order of subdiaconate as a positive move. Do you agree with the author's conclusion? Do you feel that since lay people have taken over many of the roles once assigned to those in minor orders and subdiaconate, that these offices are obsolete? Discuss.

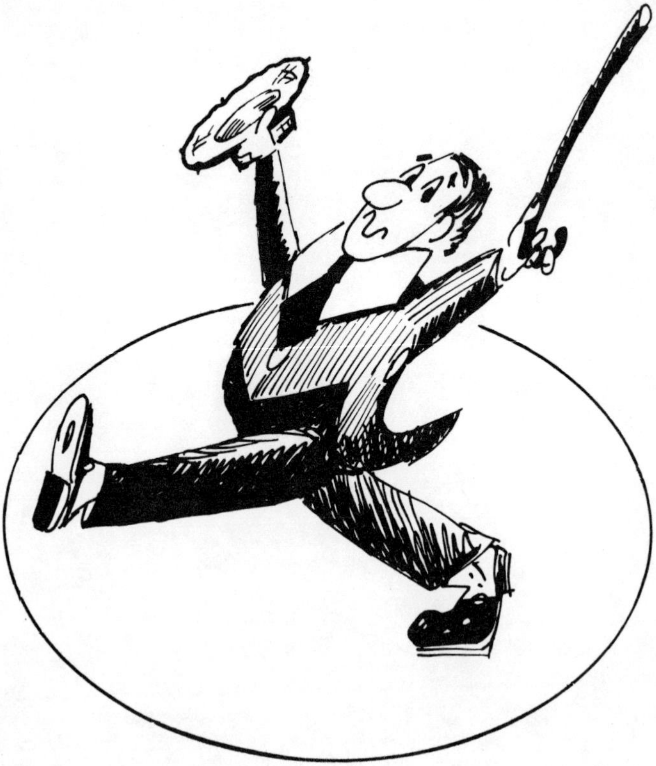

WHAT'S HAPPENING TO CONSCIENCE?

BY LEONARD FOLEY, O.F.M.

Poor conscience! It used to be a "still, small voice" at the back of our heads. Now it's been pulled into the open. It's a star on the morality stage, with all sorts of press agents, spotlight publicity and catchy slogans. Sometimes, like a "created" movie star, it must want to go out into the audience and shout, "Hey, I'm still the same *me*! I'm still what I always was, down on the farm!"

It's the slogans that cause the misunderstanding. For instance, "You can form your own conscience." As sometimes quoted, this seems to imply that you couldn't form your own conscience *before*, but now you *can*—credit probably due to Pope John. Or, to take another slippery catch phrase, "It's up to *you* to decide whether something is right or wrong." True, indeed. God said that to Adam the first day he sent him out to get Eve some breakfast. "Use your head, Adam. Don't be expecting me to be passing you notes every half hour, telling you to turn left, take a nap or swim to Afghanistan. You have intelligence and you're free and you know who I am. Be a man!" What God also said was, "When you're deciding, Adam, start with what I've done and said, with facts, with reality."

A Mature Christian Conscience—What's That?

The word *mature* in this title is a cop-out, because what's worrying parents today is how their children *acquire* a mature Christian conscience. There's no denying that this is a serious problem; it always has been. But it's a problem of *education,* of a process. In this article we're concerned with what the end result of the education is supposed to be. Growing up to what? What is a good home supposed to produce? We have to consider *what* we're trying to achieve before we can decide *how* to do it.

A mature Christian conscience may be called the other side of the coin of mature Christian faith. To know what conscience is, we need to consider the attitude of a person who has reached the basic decision to give himself totally to Christ.

This, as we saw in the article on sin, is something we grow into gradually. We come to a basic decision for or against God's offer of friendship. Faith is the across-the-board acceptance of God's offer of intimate and eternal friendship through Christ. Our response is not perfect (venial sinfulness continues), but it is deep enough to be called a fundamental decision about our whole life. Over a period of time a person realizes that God is calling him to a total relationship, one that comes ahead of all other relationships. Faith is man *responding.*

What's Happening to Conscience?

Long- And Short-Range Conscience

An important distinction must be made here. We are talking about two kinds of response:

1) The response that determines the *direction* of one's whole life. We see something similar to this kind of basic, long-range decision every day: the mutual commitment of two people to marry; the response of a Peace Corpsman who gives two years of his life; that of a man who volunteers for four years in the army; the response of a football player signing to play for a certain team; the response of an artist invited to design a beautiful building. These are *overall* responses, general and all-determining; they are not concerned with particular actions.

So also in a mature Christian there is an *overall faith* and an *overall conscience,* a fundamental decision about life. When a man and woman marry, they cannot know every detail of the life they will live; they are ready—overall—to give their loving response as individual situations indicate. The wife does not know that in six years she'll be called upon to take care of an invalid husband. A nun does not know when she takes her vows that she will have to represent her community in a school crisis, but she is ready for whatever comes. So a mature Christian is one who is fundamentally ready to respond in love to God without knowing what all the particular responses will be.

2) There are the *particular,* short-range conscience decisions carrying out our basic decision in concrete detail, day by day, action by action. These are all the daily responses of husband and wife; all the decisions the quarterback makes; all the helpful things the Peace Corpsman actually decides to do; all the drawings of the artist.

A Privilege, Not A Burden

Before we consider the matter of particular responses, we might do well to pause to realize the dignity involved in this *ability to respond freely* to God. God puts us, in a sense, on a par with himself. It is true that he *demands* a response,

Keeping Up with Our Catholic Faith

but it is not the cold decree of a tyrant. It is the insistence of one who can make us happy forever. Even within the absolute command of God, we are free. He made us like himself: we couldn't be happy or do ourselves eternal good if we weren't doing things freely. If it isn't my choice, it isn't me; and if it isn't me, I'm not happy. So even within God's "must," there is freedom. Vatican II says, "God has respect for the dignity of the human person he created. Man is to be guided by his own judgment and he is to enjoy freedom."

Enter Quarterback Kolinsky

"General" and "particular" conscience can be illustrated in a hero we'll now create: Quarterback Kolinsky. He too has made a "basic decision." Because he wants to play football and play it well, he signs the contract offered him by the Oregon Oleos and commits himself to play football for them for three years. How does he carry out his basic decision? First, *he faces reality*. This includes many decisions before he gets near the field. a) He accepts some *absolutes:* there are boundary lines that never move, goalposts between which the ball must fly, 10-yard measuring chains that are unshrinkable and unstretchable; there are only 3,600 seconds in the game. b) He accepts some *general directions* from the coach: we don't pass on the side where the All-American linebacker is playing; we don't try a reverse with slow-moving Joe Stutz; we don't "go for it" on fourth down. c) Quarterback Kolinsky *studies the usual* situation. He looks at films of the other team, reads scouting reports. He learns the skills and limitations of his own players. So now he has absolutes, general directions and information.

"Reading" The Situation

Now Quarterback Kolinsky faces the *reality of the moment*. When he goes back to pass on the first play, there are three or four men he can possibly throw to. He has to "read" the situation: how well each pass-receiver is "covered;" the relative danger of interception. In three or four seconds he must decide to throw to 1, 2, 3 or 4, to run, or be "sacked." He decides as best he can, remembering the absolutes, the gen-

What's Happening to Conscience?

eral directions, the background information and the facts of the moment.

This is what a mature Christian does. He knows the absolutes, the general principles of the faith; he "reads" the circumstances of the present as best he can; he makes a decision.

If there's an extra-speedy defender that Quarterback Kolinsky wasn't told about and his pass gets intercepted, his decision was still a prudent one. So also, if a Christian's conscientious decision turns out "wrong" because of something not under his control, unforeseen, it's still a good decision of conscience before God.

So the conscience of a Christian is an enlightened conscience. 1) It is enlightened in *general.* The Christian has accepted Christ as the basic value of his life. He knows Christ, what he said and did. He knows at least in general the wisdom of centuries of experience by the Church; he knows in general what the guides and leaders of the Church have to say to him. He knows the law. He knows what is fatal to his purpose, what is dangerous. 2) *In particular,* the Christian tries to be enlightened about the present situation: who is involved, what the personalities and needs are; what the alternatives and consequences of various actions will be. When he has given enough time to considering these motives, he makes a decision as to what God wants him to do *here and now.* He is at least implicitly carrying out his commitment to Christ.

Quarterback Kolinsky may decide not to use the play the coach ordered because Fullback Nelson, who was to carry the ball, tells him in the huddle that his leg is injured, and there is no chance to take a time-out. So the quarterback decides on another play to carry out the overall purpose of the game—to move the ball, to win.

So, a housewife decides that now is the time to see her neighbor about the dog's running through her flower bed. A college student decides that now is the time to speak up in class. A priest decides to drop his prepared homily and speak with an eye on an incident that happened just before Mass and which has affected the whole congregation. Conscience is a decision to respond to God in a way that fits the present situation. It takes into consideration both the general directions of the law and all concrete factors.

Sure You're Creative!

You and I don't think we're creative. We don't use the word, at least. But if we love someone, we are always thinking up ways to do them good, to please them. So it is with an enlightened conscience: it is also creative.

For an everyday comparison, let's leave Quarterback Kolinsky with his problems and consider the relationship of husband and wife. They are, in a way that is at least similar to our faith-relationship to God through Christ, committed to love each other *basically* and *in detail.*

They love each other. But how? The sixth commandment tells them only what *not* to do; it does not tell them what particular decisions to make. If they really love each other, they don't ask, "What do I *have* to do for you?" Rather, they think up ways of pleasing each other: something special for dinner, the suggestion of a trip, a gift, a going out of the way to be considerate, patient, helpful. They are, much of the time at least, improvising in a positive creative way.

The enlightened conscience is also alert for what will make any situation *good*—for God, for others, for oneself. Perhaps *imaginative* or *sensitive* would be just as good a word as *creative.* A good person is alert not only to the factors of a situation (enlightened) but also to the *possibilities* (creative). A friend doesn't just decide that now is *not* the time to talk about the other's hangups; she searches for alternatives: just listening quietly, suggesting a walk or a movie; showing her a new dress; telling her about a book she's reading; or deciding that the other had best be left alone just now.

People with creative consciences get into the habit of *enrich-*

What's Happening to Conscience?

ing situations—making them occasions of fun, or encouragement, or sympathy, or peace. Father Albert Jonsen says, "The responsible man as decision-maker is aware that the values he accepts must be realized in *new* situations and *new* difficulties, with *renewed* energy and resourcefulness."

When Laws Conflict

We have seen the realism of Quarterback Kolinsky facing the actual situation when he tries to pass. There is another kind of realism we must sometimes have: when laws *conflict*, and when circumstances make it actually or morally impossible to do more than the minimum. When two laws demand opposite actions, the enlightened and creative Christian asks: Which is more important right now? Which one should I obey to carry out God's saving and healing purpose right now?

So, for instance, Quarterback Kolinsky decides not to use the play the coach has just ordered from the bench because Fullback Nelson, who was to carry the ball, tells him in the huddle that his leg is injured. There is no chance for a time-out, so Kolinski quickly decides to pass. He is taking the "higher" of two conflicting laws: He's safeguarding Fullback Nelson's physical well-being (the law of justice and charity).

Or, Charlie Wilson has a friend in the hospital who is terribly upset and desperately needs companionship. But Charlie also has an appointment in another city to consider a new job that will relieve the great financial distress his family is suffering. He decides that he must leave his friend and go see about the job.

Or, Al Beamer knows that he should support his family with a reasonable income. But the job that is providing his present income is keeping him away from home so much that his marriage is being strained to the breaking point. He decides that it is more important to change jobs, take a lower income and spend more time with his family.

A man knows that he should preserve his life. But he knows that his death will liberate untold millions. So he walks into

Jerusalem, where he knows that he will be captured and put to death.

Some laws admit of no conflict, it is true—the absolutes. Absolutely I must love God, my neighbor and myself. But any positive individual action I must do may be deferred, omitted for the present for serious reasons. But the *negative laws of God* admit of no exceptions. One cannot commit adultery or directly kill the innocent *for any reason.* But apart from the absolutes, traditional moral theology has always held that I can and must make an enlightened and creative decision to let a higher law (for instance, charity or justice) have its way over a conflicting lesser law, even an important one.

Limited Man

The other area of realism is similar. It has to do with our limitations. Sometimes, because of emotional stress, physical pain or fatigue, I simply cannot do more than the minimum. For instance, if a man has spent several hours in a tense and angry discussion at the office, he may not be able *right now* to give reasonable attention to his wife or his teenage boy at home. If a woman has exhausted herself taking care of babies all day, she can do no more than say "good night" to God before going to bed. The man who has been slandered out of a job can scarcely be expected to do more than refrain from revenge for a while.

It is because of the limitations of man that moral theologians face the question of when one "isn't obliged." They are trying to reassure good people that sometimes there are worthy reasons for doing no more than the minimum. Or, put another way: at times the minimum may be the best I can do. If one seeks out these "minimal" opinions in a desire to get out of as much as possible, he's riding a horse backwards.

The enlightened and creative conscience can sincerely say that, although under other circumstances I would gladly do more, I simply cannot do more than this now, and indeed I should not. And I know that if my friends can understand this, God surely can.

What's Happening to Conscience?

**Conscience: Not "Fixed" But Free;
Not Automatic, But Personal**

Enlightened, creative, realistic, a genuine conscience is always looking for a way to please God and is ready to carry out a basic commitment in detail. It goes without saying that one with such a conscience makes a *free* choice. No matter how much external circumstances thwart or destroy my capacity for action, I can always make an internal decision freely. (Of course, if someone drugs or tortures me into unconsciousness, I am not making any human decisions at all.) As Doctor Victor Frankl says in reference to people in the Nazi concentration camps, "I can always exercise the last of human freedoms: I can *choose my attitude* in any set of circumstances."

Another way of saying that conscience is free and human is to say that it is a *personal* choice. No one else can decide for husband and wife what they ought to do for each other every day to deepen or even preserve their love. Two friends do not need, and could not tolerate, someone giving them a "program" outlining in detail what they should say to each other all day long.

So it is with conscience. When all the facts are in, all the awareness of the will of God and the law of man, my act must be *my* decision, something that *I* myself choose to do, something I stand behind. It is not enough to be in a church building on Sunday; I must choose to worship God personally. No one can say my prayers or make my act of faith or contrition—not my mother or father, not my friend, not the pope.

This has been an attempt to describe the mature Christian conscience—or rather, the ideal Christian conscience towards which we are trying to grow. Even though we have made our basic decision for Christ, we realize that this decision must be enriched, purified, deepened, protected. It should be obvious that there is nothing "new" about this idea. This is what God gave man the dignity and power to do and to be when he first put him on the earth. We may indeed be faced with much more *complex* decisions of conscience today. But

Keeping Up with Our Catholic Faith

conscience itself is still the same. Even in the spotlight of new discussion, conscience still wants to come out into the audience and say, "Hey, I'm still the same me."

Finally, conscience is the basic decision, gradually arrived at, to give oneself totally to the Father through Christ; it is alertness to ways of carrying out this commitment in actual circumstances of life; it is the concrete making of decisions that are enlightened, creative and realistic; decisions of free and loving sons and daughters of the Father.

Questions for Discussion

1. No one is ever "finished" maturing; but we've all made some basic decisions that "predate" individual actions. Can you identify some of the basic decisions that you live by? How do these compare with "general" and "particular" conscience?

2. Is it possible to sense something as wrong without being able to express exactly why it is wrong? How reliable is such a feeling?

3. What factors do you consider in judging the morality of a situation? Is it possible to follow your conscience and still be dead wrong? How?

4. Cite examples of positive obligations one may have but be forced by necessity to omit for a time. Find other examples of negative (i.e., prohibiting) laws of God which admit of no exception for any reason.

5. Can one have a greater or lesser degree of freedom in, say, being honest, obedient, law-abiding? When is freedom so diluted that the act is no longer credited or charged to me? Is conscience automatically translating a law into action?

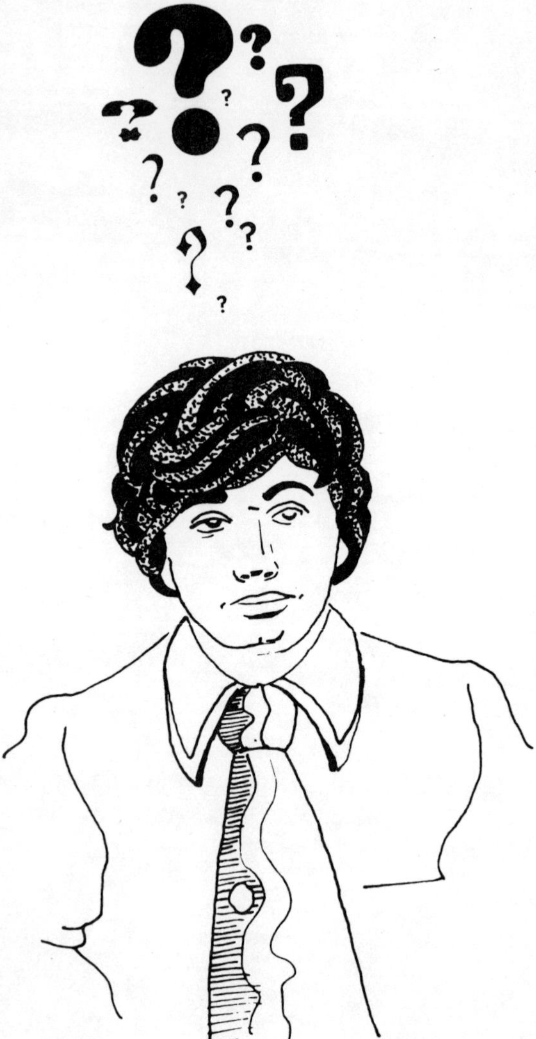

ISN'T ANYTHING A SIN ANYMORE?

BY LEONARD FOLEY, O.F.M.

Many Catholics feel that the rug has been pulled out from under them in the last 10 years. It used to be, people say, that you could get a straight answer from a priest. There were laws and rules, strict dogmas and authority. If you wanted to know where the Church stood on missing Mass, daily prayer, practicing rhythm, going to "B" movies, going steady or being a bridesmaid at a Protestant wedding, you asked a priest and he told you.

Now, some people say, you'll hear of a priest telling a mother, "I'm not sure that your boy is committing mortal sin if he misses Mass on Sunday or has those dirty paperbacks under his pillow." Or, instead of telling you that you can go

Keeping Up with Our Catholic Faith

to this or that movie, he says you'll have to make up your mind whether or not you have a good enough reason. It all sounds very fuzzy and permissive.

I think the heart of the problem lies in the fact that life has gotten very *complex*; or rather, we are *feeling the complexity* more than we formerly did. We always knew, for instance, that we had to "love our neighbor" (that sounds fairly simple), but nowadays we feel so confused and helpless about *how* to love our neighbor as we see him on TV every night: starving in Biafra, carrying a coffin in Ireland, locked into a big city slum, or cheering and heckling speakers at the U. N. We always knew that violence was wrong—except in a just war; but now it isn't so clear which wars are just.

A growing sense of complexity forces us to say, "It's very hard to decide when something is actually morally wrong, or when somebody is actually morally guilty."

SINFULNESS OR LOVE OF GOD IS OUR *WHOLE* LIFE

You come away from the funeral of Mary X. and you say, "Well, she didn't go to church much and she drank a lot; but she was good to her kids, and there was never a sick neighbor who didn't get a bowl of soup from her!" What are you saying? Simply this: there was a basic goodness in Mary X.'s life that was not destroyed by certain acts or omissions that *could* be mortally sinful but in her case didn't seem to be.

Another case: Some things seem to be perfectly correct, and yet they don't add up to what life is supposed to be. John Y. goes to Mass every Sunday, fulfills all his money obligations, doesn't get drunk and never steals even a pencil at work. But he seems to have no concern at all for the feelings of his wife; his children fear and resent him; he refuses to give help to any person or any cause. We are tempted to think that there is something deeply wrong with his life, in spite of the fact that he keeps (some of) the commandments.

Or take the case of those good friends of yours who

Isn't Anything a Sin Anymore?

are "married outside the Church." They love each other and their children very much. Their home is practically a "welcome center" in the neighborhood. They go to Mass every Sunday and cooperate in parish activities. Now, Jesus said, "The man who marries a divorced woman likewise commits adultery." Yet you find it simply impossible to believe that this couple is "living in sin."

What are we inclined to conclude from these instances? First, that the *internal attitude* of a person may not be as good or as bad as the external action indicates. It's what's inside that counts. Second, there is more to being a good or bad person than a certain number of external actions. Again, morality seems to lie in an ongoing, overall attitude, deep inside the person.

Therefore, I'm trying to emphasize in this article that mortal sinfulness is primarily an *interior attitude,* a profound, inner decision about life.

And because of the *internalness* of sin, it is extremely difficult—personally I think it is impossible—to judge that *somebody else* is guilty of mortal sinfulness.

Our plan will be to carry to its logical conclusions that traditional threefold test of mortal sinfulness: serious matter, full knowledge, full consent.

WHAT IS *T-H-E* "SERIOUS MATTER" ABOVE ALL OTHER "SERIOUS MATTERS"?

To understand mortal sinfulness, let's start with the opposite: love of God. If serious sin is "mortal," that is, "death-producing, fatal," then the opposite—love of God— must be "life-producing, healing, healthful." So we can test love of God in corresponding terms. To love God genuinely (to "commit" love-of-God) three things are necessary: serious matter, full knowledge, full consent.

Sounds "different," doesn't it? But can we say anything less? Must not something eternally good be as "serious"

Keeping Up with Our Catholic Faith

in a positive way as mortal sin is "serious" in a negative way?

What may strike us first is that it's hard to think of *a* love of God, as we sometimes speak of *a* mortal sin. We either love God or we don't, basically. Does this begin to make clear that love of God (as well as its opposite, mortal sin) is an *all-the-time* matter, an attitude, something in our hearts before it appears on the outside?

What we're talking about, of course, is the primary commandment that underlies all other commandments: "You must love the Lord your God with all your heart, with all your soul, and with all your mind. This is the greatest and the first commandment. The second resembles it: You must love your neighbor as yourself. On these two commandments the whole law is based" (Matthew 23:37).

This is *the* "serious matter" that comes before any individual "serious matter." In this primary commandment God is not asking us to send food to Biafra, or go to Mass on Sunday. He is asking for *a total giving of our life to him, our whole life all the time, inside and outside.*

Theologians call this our "fundamental option." It is our fundamental decision about life itself, not (yet) about individual situations. It is a basic, core commitment. For Christians, it is centered on Christ, who makes the offer of the Father visible to us. It is a total Yes to him. It is absolute. "He who is not with me is against me."

Now, for anyone committed to Christ in this way, there are all kinds of very serious ways of expressing this love *externally:* being concerned about others' housing, welcoming people to a parish, listening to someone in trouble, celebrating the Eucharist and the other sacraments, feeding a baby, etc. These are all "serious." Just when or how they are to be carried out is not the absolute. Rather the meaning beneath the surface is what is absolute: love of God and man. I may judge that staying with someone is more seriously required by charity *right now* than going to Sunday Mass *right now,* even though the latter is also seriously required by love of God. In either case *the* serious matter of total love of God is not affected. It is simply carried out in a different way.

WHAT IS *T-H-E* MORTAL SINFULNESS BENEATH ALL INDIVIDUAL MORTAL SINS?

What is it that destroys this "fundamental option" of love of God? Obviously the exact opposite. If love of God is a basic, core commitment to Christ and the Father, mortal sinfulness is a basic, core refusal of commitment. It is a decision about life itself: life will *not* be given totally to God, but to myself, to lesser values. This is *the* mortal sin before all other mortal sins. It is not, indeed, just *a* mortal sin but an attitude, an *all-the-time* internal, basic attitude.

It is the overall attitude that comes before any particular sin. Long before a man commits cold-blooded murder, he has made a life-decision that *no* commandment of God will stand in the way of what he wants. Long before hatred hardens into cold-blooded slander, there is a basic willingness to reject the basic call of God to imitate him. In other words, it would seem that only after someone arrives at a real "mortal sin attitude" is he capable of any individual mortal sin. His "mortal attitude" precedes and underlies his external sin of murder or slander.

When the catechism says that something must be "serious" to be a mortal sin, it means that certain actions *are presumed* to express the person's total rejection of God. It means that these actions cannot coexist with the total love of God which is faith. And we must immediately add that one must *realize* this seriousness. As the catechism says, "seriously wrong or *considered* seriously wrong." I cannot be innocent, no matter what excuses and rationalizations I employ, if I really consider something seriously wrong; i.e., the expression of an attitude that means turning away from God in a basic way. By the same token, I cannot be guilty, no matter what I do, if in complete honesty and openness to God I really do not consider something seriously wrong.

WHAT ABOUT "FULL KNOWLEDGE" AND "FULL CONSENT"?

Have you noticed that we weren't able to talk about "serious matter" without getting into the matter of knowledge, awareness and consent?

Obviously, one can love God with his "whole mind" only if his whole mind knows what is going on. I can't be responsible one way or the other if I don't know about the God I'm accepting or rejecting, or if I don't know the *meaning* of the act I perform or omit. Equally obviously, I am not responsible one way or the other if what I do is not *my decision,* freely made in reference to *what I am aware of.* I get no "credit" for what I do not choose; I have no guilt for what I do not choose.

We have seen that mortal sinfulness (like love) is an attitude. An attitude is an ongoing decision, a habitual *frame of mind.* It is a whole *outlook* on life. Mortal sinfulness includes the *realization* that there is an offer from God of a total union of life and happiness with him and that I am (gradually, indeed) rejecting this offer across the board, basically. It is obvious, but let us say it: I cannot totally reject God unless I *somehow* realize what I am doing.

And again, I cannot separate myself from God unless I'm the one who does it. Me. My free choice. Nobody else can force me, persuade me, seduce me: if it's not my fully free decision, it's not mortal sinfulness, no matter what else it is.

HOW LONG DOES IT TAKE TO MAKE A BASIC DECISION?

One more factor must be considered: no decision or action is *isolated* from what went before. Even an impetuous or rash action has a history or attitude of impetuosity behind it. As living, thinking human beings, we go by steps—the literal meaning of *gradual.*

First, *in coming to our basic decision about life*—love

Isn't Anything a Sin Anymore?

of God or mortal sinfulness. When is a person capable of making a basic decision, for good or ill, about *the* serious matter of life? By definition, a baby, a child is not mature. A teenager? When? At 13, 15, 17?

The canon law of the Church says that a marriage *can* be valid when the boy is 16 and the girl 14. Civil law usually puts the age further back. In my state a boy must be 18 and a girl 16 to get a marriage license, and then only with parents' or court's permission; otherwise the age is 21. There are similar age requirements for drivers' licenses. So, common human wisdom says that mature judgment, the ability to make a serious decision, is something one reaches only gradually.

Second, a basic attitude or decision about life, and about lesser serious commitments in life, develops only *gradually*. A doctor decides to give up his practice only after months, perhaps years. Husbands and wives only gradually grow to the point where they do not, in fact, love each other. No one becomes an alcoholic, a Communist, or a Christian in one moment. People pray and think and listen for months or years before taking the step of seeing a priest or minister about "joining a Church." People do not really fall in and out of love in a day or a week.

In other words, life has *momentum* that is not instantaneously changed. It's more like the movement of a great ship on the ocean. The ship can't stop on a dime and reverse itself or even dash off at a perfect right angle. So also, *people do not zigzag in and out of mortal sinfulness or total love of God* like a broken-field runner in football. One does not commit *a* mortal sin at 3 o'clock, go to confession at 5, commit "another" mortal sin at 7, go to confession at 9, etc. Must we not say of one who seems to do this that either there has been no real mortal sinfulness or no real repentance?

SUMMING UP

To return to our original problem: Why do the answers of some priests and some mothers and fathers seem to be "fuzzy" and "permissive" as regards the sinfulness of certain actions? It would seem that they are simply more *aware* than we perhaps used to be that judging another person's interior moral guilt is extremely complex and difficult, and, I believe, impossible.

Also, the new moral perspective places more accent on Christlike *understanding* than on Pharisee-like *judging*, one of the few things Jesus severely condemned. It doesn't say that nothing is a sin anymore. But it does try to push sin back where it belongs—deep in the decision-making region of our being. And thus the attitude of the heart gets more attention than, say, a slap of the hand or a slip of the tongue.

The "basic attitude" approach also seems more in line with Christian hope. One is less likely to despair if he sees sin not so much as a sudden nose dive into decadence but as a gradual and complex decision about the direction of his life and the quality of his relationships. Where would the Good News of Christ be if one could lose everything on a moment's impulse?

Christian hope tells us that Jesus' victory over sin has started the momentum in our favor. It also tells us that a person's core commitment to follow Christ will not be readily reversed or disturbed by failures located more on the outer rim of his experience. Such an outlook encourages the Christian, despite his failures, to spend more time atuning himself to the power of Christ in the world than in lying awake at night whining over his guilt. It likewise makes it easier to believe the best about others and about ourselves and to affirm the Good News of Jesus: "Have confidence, I have overcome the world."

Isn't Anything a Sin Anymore?

Questions for Discussion

1. Name complex moral situations, other than the ones discussed in the text, that confront you today. Can we judge the extent of guilt (sinfulness) in another person? Can we judge the goodness or badness of an act in itself?

2. Think of some cases of apparently good actions that are contradicted by other bad conduct in an imaginary person. Which of the two "apparent" persons is the real person? How would you define mortal sin?

3. The Bible compares love of God with married love. How are the two loves similar? How are they different?

4. Take some everyday actions and try to decide the ultimate motive underlying them. Why does a man go to work? Why does the woman answer the phone with a pleasant voice? Why does the pickpocket size up everybody on the street? Are these cases of "total commitment"?

5. Discuss the statement "It's all right if you think it's all right." Do you agree that basic mortal sinfulness in attitude precedes any external mortal sin?

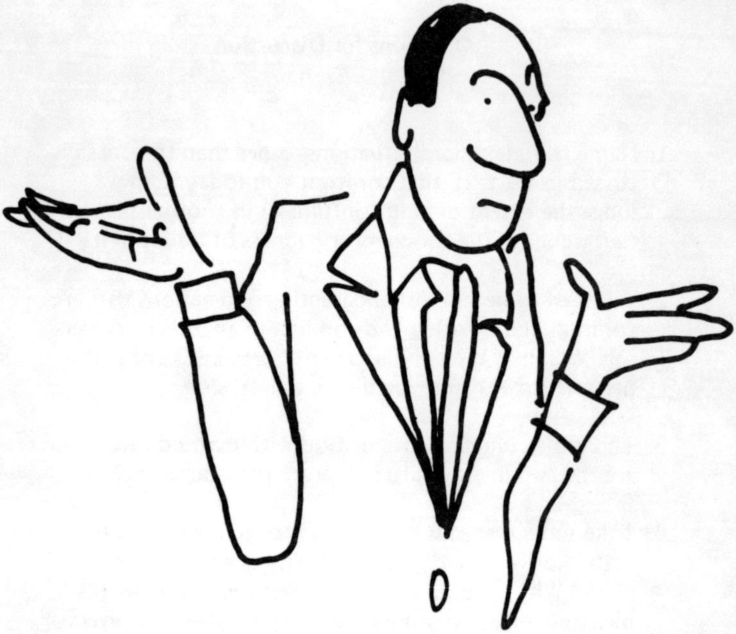

WHY DON'T THEY TEACH THE TEN COMMANDMENTS ANYMORE?

BY LEONARD FOLEY, O.F.M.

Who ever would have thought that the Ten Commandments and "love" could become opponents on a religious education battlefield? Well, maybe the word "battlefield" is rather strong; "area of tension" is perhaps a better phrase.

Many parents feel that their children are not being taught the Ten Commandments by those (outside the home) who teach religion; many complain that the children have not memorized the Ten Commandments. On the other hand, many Catholic teachers point out that the core of Christian moral life is to love God and love one's neighbor as Jesus did; that this includes the Ten Commandments, and that it goes far beyond them.

Keeping Up with Our Catholic Faith

No doubt, as the old lubricative has it, "There is much to be said for both sides." But there must be some way of alleviating the tension. It may be over-ambitious, but that is the purpose of this chapter.

Is There Something Deeper Involved?

Obviously no one knows what is being taught in every one of the 8,800 Catholic grade schools and 1,800 high schools, and the CCD programs of possibly 18,000 parishes. And I haven't read through the several sets of religion texts being used through grades 1-12. But I can testify to my being mightily impressed by studying the "scope and sequence" charts of several of these textbook series. I could only say to myself, "If these kids really absorb all this content over that period of time, they must be the best instructed students in our history."

Be that as it may, many parents feel their children are not being taught rightly on many scores, the commandments included. Having listened to many of them in adult education discussions, I have come to the opinion that their complaint about the commandments is *also* the symbol or focus of many worries about their own life. It is a symbol of the *haziness* that seems to have taken over morality; everything is so complex and complicated. It is a symbol of the *loss of discipline*, "strictness," of the flabbiness and affluence which seem to have taken over modern society. It is a symbol of what seems to them a dangerous *freedom* that disregards law when it is convenient to do so—a freedom of thought and action that has come to be labeled "permissiveness." It is a symbol of *nostalgia* for "the good old days" of simpler faith, when, many think, we did not have many views in theology, or shifting emphases. Lastly, it seems to be a protest against a generalized (and therefore impractical) "love" that talks a good game but doesn't get around to doing things.

The Explosion Of Change

If there is any merit to this theory, then the problem would

Why Don't They Teach the Ten Commandments Anymore?

not be solved by returning, say, to the Baltimore Catechism. The problem is the great "change" that has come over the whole world—and therefore the Church. And the changing world has exerted a confusing influence on our children— the flood of values constantly poured into their experience by the all-encompassing world of TV, records, paperbacks, newspapers—the values of a frankly non-Christian society.

One suspects, then, that the arguement is not really about the Ten Commandments, but about the whole frightening problem of passing on values to children in a society that is increasingly counteracting these values with those of a consumer society, affluent, self-sufficient, godlike in technology, untrammeled in expression in art and literature, entertainment-happy, etc.

Perhaps parents will understand, then, that leaders in religious education are trying to cope with a *world* problem, with the explosion of change, and with preparing young Catholics to become responsible adults with values that will keep them on an even keel in a world that will give them little or no support for their Christian beliefs and values. They are trying to "give" them the Ten Commandments *and a lot more*—an experience of and conviction about Christianity itself: or, to be quite practical: a personal relationship with Jesus which is the only thing that will last through a lifetime of testing.

The Strength Of The New Approach

There's nothing new under the sun. But the development of catechetics in recent decades, greatly aided by the biblical renewal as well as a greater awareness in child psychology, has resulted in a unified view of what it means to be a Christian. There is a great stress on meaning, and value, besides external practice. It seems to have been inevitable that in a world where a million facts, rumors, denials, whispers, claims, are being poured over our heads every day, people (children) would ask with greater need than ever before; "What, of all this, is really important? What's really valuable? What's first, what's second? Why? What's the meaning? What's it all about?"

Keeping Up with Our Catholic Faith

So the emphasis has been on the *one* story of God's dealing with us and its *meaning.* God is one who loved us eternally in Christ, and decided to share his very life with us, so that we could enjoy his happiness forever. Jesus is the eternal model of all the sons and daughters he would have. When mankind sinned, he did not change his plan, but became redeemer too. Jesus came among us, and showed us how to live the human-divine life God always wanted us to have— and to live this way in spite of suffering, hate, sin, cruelty. "He who sees me sees the Father."

So God calls man, invites him, almost pleads with him to accept the gift of eternal life. Man's life, therefore, is simply response to God. He loves God in return, with the power of God's own Spirit within him, in the imitation of the human-divine Jesus. The overall, simple (and terribly difficult) response is *love—love of God, others, self,* not just any old way, but *as Jesus did.* This is the overall disposition of the Christian. It is based on an *experience* of Jesus, and therefore of the Father and his Spirit, as the incarnate love of God, and a vision of his goodness and love. The response is made in the visible Body which Christ gathered together to be the continuing sign of his love—the Church. The Church is the group of men and women who know that they share a common vocation, a common life, a common Father, and a common love.

This may sound visionary, but it is Christianity. Nothing could be more ideal than God's own plan. The picture includes sin, evil, suffering, death, Satan, the possibility of eternal loss. The very beauty of the plan is an obvious condemnation of anything that would spoil it.

The Weakness Of An Over-all General Approach

All well and good. I won't do anything very long without reasons. I will keep up "practices" only if they have meaning. I am a mature Christian only if I have a personal relationship with Christ. I can't live on laws if I don't have deep values.

Why Don't They Teach the Ten Commandments Anymore?

But Christ also said, "By their fruits will you know them," and "Not those who say to me 'Lord, Lord,' will enter the kingdom of heaven, but those who do the will of my Father." He called for prayer, fasting, almsgiving, rooting out the occasions of sin at any cost, prudence, watchfulness, generosity, courage, etc. etc.

There is a danger, most teachers would admit, of not getting down to brass tacks. A Christian filled with all this idealism should keep the Ten Commandments. But, as all good teachers know, things have to be spelled out—or specifically figured out by the student. So the Ten Commandments of Christ have to be spelled out too. It *is* wrong for a Christian to steal, to lie, to cheat, to entertain lustful and greedy intentions, to expose himself to this and that occasion of sin, to neglect prayer. It is necessary (inevitable) for a Christian to pray, to worship alone and with others, to be a cooperative member of the body of Christ as it exists in *this* area, this group. It is necessary for a Christian to obey laws, to honor parents, to be polite, fair, honest, and chaste in actual life.

To enter into these specifics can be a valuable teaching tool—for it can mean an opportunity to show that Christian values—the presence of Christ himself—enters into the practicalities of everyday life. It will be a chance to show *why*, for instance, fornication is evil (not just a prohibition) and why prayer is good (not just a law).

The Value Of The Commandments Approach

To state the weakness of a onesided "value" approach, as we have just done, is to present the position of those who favor more emphasis on the specifics of the commandments.

We are not spirits, but human beings. Our souls have a skin, so to speak, and we communicate with each other only by visible signs. If, then, the name of the game is relationship in love, the communication of this love has to be *visible* or it is not human. What merely stays in our head isn't really human—not really real, as we learn when a showdown comes for a "conviction" we thought we had.

Keeping Up with Our Catholic Faith

The very foundation of the sacraments—indeed of the very Incarnation of Jesus—is that we need to see, hear, taste, touch. That's the way we are, as human beings.

This means details, particulars. There is no such thing as "generally" loving somebody. I love him through what I *do*, visibly. I look at him with respect, I listen to him, I give him something with my hand, I touch him, I respect his physical "area" as being the concrete sign of his whole person.

So it is human and understandable that parents are concerned about what their children *do* and don't *do*. Whether or not they do steal the butter in the supermarket, whether they do express their prayerful attitude in words and action; whether their loving God above all things includes joining the Christian community at Sunday Mass; whether "love" includes respecting the body of as well as the "person"; whether or not Johnny knows the prayer Christ gave us.

Even a pagan world shrewdly demands that we "put our money where our mouth is," lay it on the line, "come up with something," etc. Fanaticism about details is one thing; but a wooly idealism that never quite gets around to the real world is equally disastrous.

Why Don't They Teach the Ten Commandments Anymore?

Perhaps part of the problem—related to the explosion of change—is the decision about *which* concrete practices children should be taught. Obviously, slandering, disrespecting, lying, dishonoring parents, fornicating and X-rated movies are not negotiable. But parents are sometimes worried about certain forms of devotion which are not essential. One can have a deep and fruitful friendship with the Mother of God, for instance, and not be able to sit still for five decades of the rosary. (Though, one must admit, there is little evidence of anything replacing it).

Perhaps parents may be yearning for the best of the days of novenas, First Fridays, May processions, weekly confession, and children attending Mass every day. Maybe we have lost too much. But we have not simply lost all expression. Children today will always remember their experience of "planning the liturgy," as we now say, making banners, communal celebration of the sacrament of confession, "field" trips to hospitals, "discussions" in class, early concern for world problems, early awareness (hopefully) of the wholesomeness of sex, early introduction to church music and art.

The Drawbacks Of Over-emphasizing Externals

Perhaps we get to the nub of the controversy today when we listen to teachers and theologians say that there had to be a change in our emphasis. They cite the words of Vatican II calling for a renewal of *moral theology,* the need for greater emphasis on Scripture, and a positive emphasis on the beauty of the Christian vocation to "bear fruit in charity for the good of the world."

Even the most worried parents will admit, I would think, that we did place a tremendous emphasis on externals. As we have just seen, that is important and even essential. But a one-sided emphasis on just *doing* things, without a corresponding emphasis on *reasons* and values will produce mechanical external compliance. This is not to say that all past Catholic "action" was meaningless. But in a different culture (before everybody started asking why) it was said, for instance that a good Catholic was one who "went to Mass on Sunday, didn't eat meat on Friday, sent his children to Catholic school, didn't practice birth control, supported the Church." (Good Protestants didn't drink or smoke or "run around.")

The reaction was against legalism, minimalism, and externalism. Legalism is a canonization of law for its own sake. ("It's the law, don't ask me why?") There's a law that says you have to go to Mass on Sunday. You go, even if you're half dead. On the other hand, you're guilty of missing Mass because you didn't literally fulfill the law—you were home in bed with two broken legs and scarlet fever. But you weren't at Mass! (In the confessional, the priest would say, "But that really wasn't your fault." And the penitent would say "But I *feel* better, confessing it"—a rather definite proof that somehow they had gotten into an overemphasis on the externals.)

Minimalism, on the other hand, wants to know how far I can go without committing mortal sin, which is hardly what the Good News of the Gospel is all about. How much of the Mass could one miss and still be guilty of "only" a venial sin? When are you drunk ("When you're lying down on the grass holding on to the world for dear life")? When (in terms of inches) is a piece of clothing immodest (as if it were the clothing, and not the person, that was immodest)? How much can I eat on a fast day? Which movies are O.K.? These are important questions—but if some other values are not *already present*, they are useless questions. They are concerned with piling up wood with no fire beneath it, making beautiful Cadillacs, with no gas exploding inside.

Laws are a facet of morality, but they are not morality. Laws are like the boundary lines of a football field, or the "works" of a telephone. Laws are like the banks of a river or the keyboard of a piano. There is always something deeper and bigger involved, a purpose and meaning, values and goals, people.

Absolute Laws and Nitty-gritty Cases

There are indeed absolute laws. One must absolutely love God above all things. To hate is absolutely wrong.

Why Don't They Teach the Ten Commandments Anymore?

To be greedy, selfish, lustful, vindictive, insincere, proud, to hate God, to refuse to worship him, to dishonor parents, to commit adultery, to slander, to be greedy and lustful, are absolutely wrong.

But laws don't give us positive particulars. For instance, it is one thing not to commit adultery. But how, positively, does a man love his wife? What does he do, say, not do, not say? When? Where? How do I make my elderly mother feel really loved and needed. How should I use my talents for the good of the world? What should I do about a friend who seems to be losing his faith? Shall I read this book? What should I do about the alcoholic father? Shall I volunteer for help at the hospital? What will I say after last night's argument?

But most laws are general, and cannot be absolutely applied to all circumstances. We don't seem to have any trouble deciding that "Thou shalt not kill" is not absolute—we kill people all the time, in war and in execution chambers. We don't think its wrong to take another man's bread if we are starving. We don't think its wrong to conceal the truth if another has no right to know it. And even in the old days there were reasons given when one is excused from Sunday Mass.

No concrete laws can cover the whole of my life. I need conscience to apply all the basics ones: "Be merciful," "Be honest," "Be truthful," "Love your neighbor as Jesus does." Conscience applies these general laws to the particular situation in view of *all* the values God has revealed to us.

Balancing love and law will be difficult, but surely not impossible. Any one of us can admit, on the one hand, that "man is prone to evil from his youth," and needs discipline, rules and regulations; that society must enforce its laws; that people must fulfill their obligations. On the other hand, anyone of us can admit that man is made in the image of God, and that God made him to be free, not a slave; God made him to be loving in spirit and not just observant of externals; and that the commandment that comes before all the others (and must be learned before them) is "Love God with your whole heart, and your neighbor as yourself—as Jesus did."

Keeping Up with Our Catholic Faith

Questions for Discussion

1. What is the difference between legalism and respect for law?

2. The author says, "The changing world has exerted a confusing influence on our children—the flood of values constantly poured into their experience by the all-encompassing world of TV, records, paperbacks, newspapers—the values of a frankly non-Christian society." Do you agree? What can parents do about it?

3. How has cultural change affected the individual personal responsibility of Catholics? What should be the Christian attitude toward external religious laws?

4. How would you respond to the accusation that social concern is "politics" and has nothing to do with "religion"?

5. Teaching children how to love is basic for the formation of a moral conscience. Why? How can parents develop greater self-discipline in themselves so as to better help their children develop it?

6. What human values are safeguarded by each of the Ten Commandments?

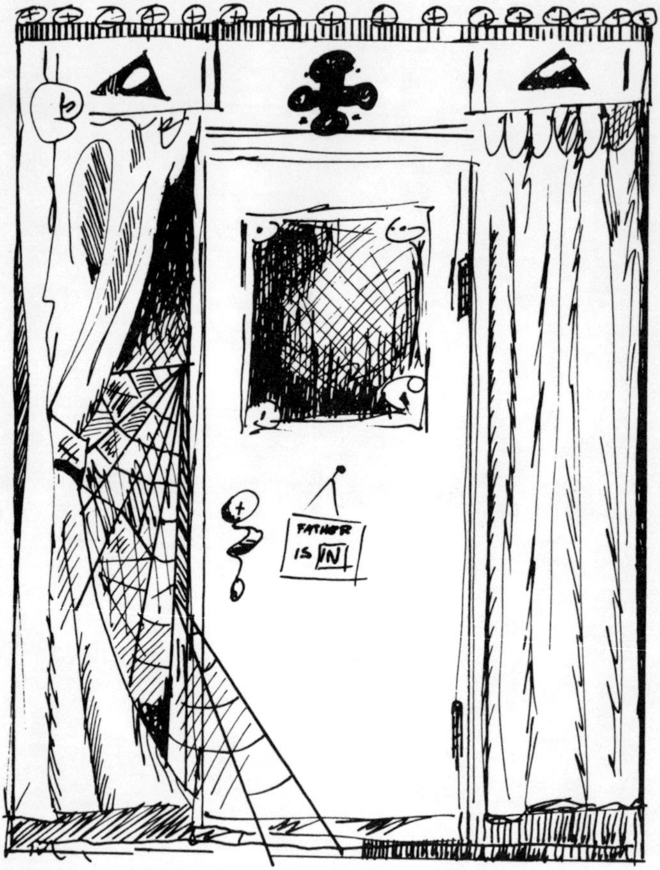
FATHER
IS IN

HAS CONFESSION GONE OUT OF STYLE?

BY LEONARD FOLEY, O.F.M.

Many Catholics today feel no need to go to confession. With the Church changing her mind on so many things, they say, how do you even know what's a sin anymore? And good, consistent advice—hmph!—where can you find that nowadays? Anyway, why should I confess my sins to a priest, to another man? Only God can forgive sins!

Right! Only God can forgive sins, because it is his friendship we have lost if we have sinned seriously. And it is our friendship with him that we have "chilled" a bit if we have sinned venially. In the end it is only a merciful God who can do what forgiving means: accept us again as his friend or let our relationship unchill.

Keeping Up with Our Catholic Faith

But the big question is: *How* does God give us his friendship? How does he restore it to us when we have lost it or damaged it? Many men at the time of Jesus jumped up and protested when the Savior said, "Go in peace, your sins are forgiven." "How dare he say this," they sniffed. "How dare this carpenter's son speak for God. Only God can forgive sins."

They could not accept God's wish that Jesus speak for him and make his mercy known in human guise—through a look, a gesture, a word filled with love that we could read and sense and feel. Yet he must have thought this very important—that we could actually hear Christ say, "You, Harold Arbuckle, are forgiven"; or that we could actually have Christ hand us a piece of bread and say, "Helen (Phyllis, Jerry), this is *me*. When you eat it, you are joined to me and to each other. I become your food and your life."

But What Happens When Jesus Can't Be Seen Anymore?

Obviously, if you have Jesus sitting down next to you, you don't need any "signs" of his acting. But when he's "gone," he must still have the purpose for which he took flesh—to be seen, and heard, and touched by his brothers and sisters, to be *God visible to men* so that they could clearly know and love him.

Christ, by his own arrangement, remains visible in other human beings called "Church," which means "the gathered-together assembly of the Lord." The Church is not merely an organization; it is the living, visible body of Christ today. To make a long story short, the Church is that group of people who are sent to stand before the world and say, "Do you want to know how kind Christ was? Look at us. Do you want to hear Christ speaking today? Listen to us. Do you want to be joined to him—or come back to him in case you deserted? Join us; rejoin us."

That's about the most conceited statement ever made, wouldn't you say? And yet that's the job the Church has. (If "Church people" ever get the notion that they're on their own in this job, then they are not only conceited but

Has Confession Gone Out of Style?

stupid.) But the fact is, Christ now has to deal with the *whole world,* not just a few people in Palestine. His resurrection is the sign that they can all come to the Father— and he must "get to" them in a human way. Once he used his own body; now he uses others'. It is still necessary that his human words be heard, that his human actions be seen— and for this he uses the human words and acts of ordinary people, like Simon, son of John, Mr. and Mrs. Everyday Smith, Paul Montini, Mary Magdalen and *you.*

What a collection! That's what St. Paul wrote to the parish in Corinth: "You're not much, guys and gals. No degree from Athens U., no pedigree back to Aristotle, no money, and what are you doing getting drunk before Mass?"

But that unimpressive group at Corinth, and your own unimpressive group, is all he's got. You're the people of God because he joined you together in Jesus. You are *one visible body.*

What has all this to do with confession? Well, just as God sent Jesus to make his life, his love and his forgiveness real in the world—something we could see, touch and feel—so Christ has sent this one visible body of ordinary men and women called the Church to make the love and the forgiveness of God real to all men.

Ideally, the sacrament of penance was the Christian community, through the bishop, welcoming back someone who had publicly sinned in a serious way. It was the visible Church carrying out the mercy of Christ saying, "Whose sins you forgive, they are forgiven. I forgive them through you." Baptism was the Father setting a new place at his table; confession is the Father welcoming back the prodigal son and having a party to celebrate the reconciliation.

What's All This "Communal" Business?

The recent emphasis on the community celebration of the sacrament of penance is the logical conclusion from thinking of the Church as a visible community. Certainly we still have to admit *our own* sins in personal confession. But sin is not just a private matter, anymore than its opposite: love of God and man. Why shouldn't we come together *as penitents*, just as we come together as members of God's family table, or welcome a new member at baptism, or gather for a wedding or funeral?

In communal celebration we come together to hear the word of God (sympathizing with our misery in sin, offering his healing) and to respond in prayers and psalms of penance, admission of sinfulness, and expressions of trust, hope and joy. There are litany-like petitions for forgiveness and prayers of thanksgiving. At the present time, except in cases of urgent necessity, "general absolution" may not be given. Each of us, if we choose to receive the sacrament, must confess personally to a priest.

But the communal emphasis says, "I don't just sin privately. I poison my whole attitude, at least a little, by any real sinfulness. And my sinful vindictiveness, selfishness, self-pity, laziness, exclusiveness—they all hurt others, even if they don't realize it, because I'm simply not able to love them as I should." In communal celebration we are all saying to each other, "I'm sorry for all I have done (and have not done) to you. You represent all the people I live with, work with. And I accept your statement of sorrow and reconciliation." And thus we are the penitent Church. The priest is the visible Christ-center around whom the Church gathers.

Yet Even Where Two Or Three . . .

What about those two or three people in the big church going to confession on Saturday afternoon? The meaning is the same. The whole community, through the priest, is reconciling sinners to the Father and to each other.

It doesn't look like much, but God is content to work patiently through his people. He lets us grow, perhaps slowly and painfully, to the realization of what it's all about:

Has Confession Gone Out of Style?

oneness in charity. Our signs get dusty; sometimes it's hard to read the meaning. We sin and we disfigure the face of Christ in the world today. Perhaps the more we realize how "serious" even the most "venial" sinfulness is, the more we will realize the need to be healed and purified, individually and as Church, so that the world may be able to see Christ.

Okay—So How About Confession?

All right, maybe I have been away from confession for too long. Maybe I should celebrate Christ's victory over sin. Maybe I should reconcile myself visibly to him and to his community.

But what should I confess? Anyone who has cut himself off from God and community by *serious sinfulness* has no problem about "what to say." It's when we bring our *lesser sinfulness* to God that the "grocery list" problem may arise. Sometimes, judging only by what the penitent *says,* the priest is forced to ask himself whether any sin at all has been committed. For instance: "I forgot my morning prayers." Now, it simply cannot be a sin to *forget* ANYTHING (unless, of course, the forgetting is planned). Or: "I missed Mass when I was sick" (two broken legs and scarlet fever). Not a sin. "But, Father, I feel better if I confess it"—a revelation that somewhere along the line somebody scared this person into a very insecure conscience! Or: "I talked about others." (Actually, it was about Mrs. Woofer, who never gave up the floor during the whole PTA meeting, and you said, "I wish she'd shut up once in a while. She makes me tired!"—an expression of legitimate personal feeling and protest.) Finally: "I was impatient with the children." (Little Butch, two years old, pulled the tablecloth—plus cups, cold soup and assorted spaghetti—off the table and into your ironing, dousing your best white blouse with catsup, and you said, "Offspring, I *wish* you wouldn't do that!")

It seems that when we tried to express ourselves we fell into a certain "script." Perhaps, indeed, as one theologian has suggested, this innocent litany was symbolic of all the real sin in our lives. "Forgetting morning prayers" may have

Keeping Up with Our Catholic Faith

Has Confession Gone Out of Style?

meant, "I really don't pray as I know I should." "I talked about others" may have meant, "I am envious of others and try to belittle them to make myself look better."

In any case, here's a suggestion. Earlier in chapter five on sin we saw that we all, sooner or later, come to a basic decision about life. Either faith or mortal sinfulness becomes our *life*, our ongoing *attitude*, the frame of mind and heart from which we operate in all situations.

So also with venial sinfulness. There is not just this and that isolated sin; there is an attitude beneath the externals. This attitude may simply be there all the time. Various circumstances bring it to the surface. This is our sinfulness, and it is this underlying attitude that needs God's healing more than anything.

Take the Mrs. Woofer business. It's easy to pass from a legitimate anger and complaint to a mean and punitive attitude. She's not only talkative; she's smart. You resent her ability to deal so efficiently with PTA's problems. She's attractive, too, and her kids get better grades than yours do; to top it all, her husband has a better job than your husband. Only temptation, so far. But your words can have a real sting when you describe the meeting to your friend. Maybe you quote her just a bit inexactly—it makes her sound a little stupid or narrow-minded. Maybe there's just a hint that she must have some ulterior motives in all the "good" she does. Funny, you never see her in public with her husband. You heard she runs up some big bills. . . .

You're punishing Mrs. Woofer, and you know it; and you enjoy it—a little. It's not the same as your bit of rejoicing when Mannix corners and clobbers the bad guys in the basement, or Leo Durocher gets thrown out for kicking dirt on the umpire's shoes. You *mean* your meanness, and you know it.

You let your resentment grow. Naturally, you forget about Mrs. Woofer when you're preparing dinner, or bowling, or attending Mass! But there she goes by in her new car, and

Keeping Up with Our Catholic Faith

you start all over. It *can* become an attitude; it *must* become an attitude if nothing is done to stop it.

Confessing The Root Causes Of Sin

There are certain ready-made attitudes that are always sitting on our doorstep waiting to be let in. These are the "capital" sins, i.e., those which are "primary, principal, chief" sins. They are *pride, laziness, anger, greed, gluttony, lust, envy.* (If you like memory tricks, they spell "plaggle" or "G-gallep"!). Even more "primary" are the sins that violate the greatest commandment—the refusal of love to God, neighbor and self: *pride* (refusal of dependence on God), *selfishness, unkindness.*

These are at the root of all external expressions of sin. These become the sinful attitudes beneath the surface. These are the sicknesses that we need to place within the strength of Christ in confession.

Confessing Our Characteristic Sin

But each of these is a unique problem to each of us because of our particular *temperament.* For instance, "laziness" in a driving, Napoleon-type person would not mean staying in bed till noon and seldom going to work, as it would in an easy-going person; it would mean neglecting the important things of faith (prayer, concern for others) in favor of nonstop activity to reach the top.

If I want to be really healed, then, like a doctor, I must go beneath the symptoms to the root causes and to my particular temperament. What is this?

Suppose your five best friends, who know you from *A* to *Zwingli,* were asked to describe you in one sentence. They would express your most noticeable characteristic. They might say "very dynamic, forceful" or "slow, easy-going," or "a picture-straightener," or "solid, silent, deep," or "very quick to think and act." Let's suppose that you are one of the "leader" types. This quality, if it is your dominant

Has Confession Gone Out of Style?

characteristic, will be at the bottom of all the good and all the bad you do. Do they need somebody to lead the Marines, organize a dance, protest working conditions, tell off the bully? You're their man (or woman). You'll be able to lead people through fire, water, red tape and apathy. Great. We need leaders.

But you will have the vices of your virtues. You are also domineering, then. You not only run the army but you also run your wife (or husband), your children, the neighbors, and motorists on the highway. At least you'll try to. And this characteristic will be the usual source of the venial sinfulness you'll commit. When you go to confession, then, you would be getting at the source if you say something like: "I am a very domineering person. This month I have again hurt my family, the people I work with, even strangers, by bossing them, running roughshod over their feelings, getting into arguments, etc."

Same thing, every time. More or less. You're the same person, with the same basic characteristic. It's there that your battle of holiness will have to be fought, and you will have to bring your consistent weakness again and again to Christ and place yourself within his strength. You are also bringing your assets, of course. The characteristic, as such, is neither good nor bad.

We all have our characteristic trait, or combination of traits. It is here we should begin when we want to get at the heart of our lives and place before God the exact weakness that needs to be healed. It is here that we find that part of our lives which is not given to God—our ongoing, habitual attitudes of sinfulness. It's the way our particular "plaggle," selfishness and refusal to love comes out.

What to confess, then? Reality. What you know very well is wrong with your life. Not pious generalities but particular facts: *the* particular fact about you. Here are some other examples (any one of these, apart from mortal sinfulness, could be your whole confession):

Keeping Up with Our Catholic Faith

"I am very self-centered, and I simply do not think about the needs or wishes of other people. As a result, this week..." Or: "I do nothing about my impulsive nature; I let myself get involved in all sorts of statements and decisions without thinking. As a result, this month..." Or: "I have hurt my family by giving in to my moodiness and self-pity." Or: "I am causing trouble at home and at the office because I don't curb my tendency to dominate other people. For instance..." Or: "I have allowed a great amount of hostility to take over my life, and I have punished and hurt many people because of it."

For some people, the simple confession of "unified" sinfulness will suffice, together with some words of encouragement from the confessor. Others will want to talk over their spiritual life and be helped by the priest to seek out means to understand themselves better, use their dominant characteristic to grow in faith and love, and to make particular decisions to avoid their usual fault.

In any case, however, the sacrament of confession can be a source of spiritual growth, a coming closer to God and a growing in his love, a coming closer to the family of men as children of God in Christ by means of this gentle and healing touch of forgiveness and love.

Has Confession Gone Out of Style?

Questions for Discussion

1. It's not easy to distinguish between involuntary feelings of resentment and freely-chosen attitudes of unkindness. Name some criteria for telling the difference.

2. Without discussing any one person, try to identify some common dominant characteristics which individuals have. Try to work out both the good and the bad that result from such a personality trait.

3. Discuss: "Confession isn't important for the person who has no more than venial sins to confess."

4. The new rite of Confession includes a communal penance service as one way of celebrating the sacrament. Why is it fitting and important that a group of friends celebrate the Sacrament of Penance together?

5. The new rite of Confession continues to require the penitent to confess his sins to a priest. Discuss why the nature of the Church requires that this practice be maintained.

6. What might the fact that "I always confess the same thing" indicate to me?

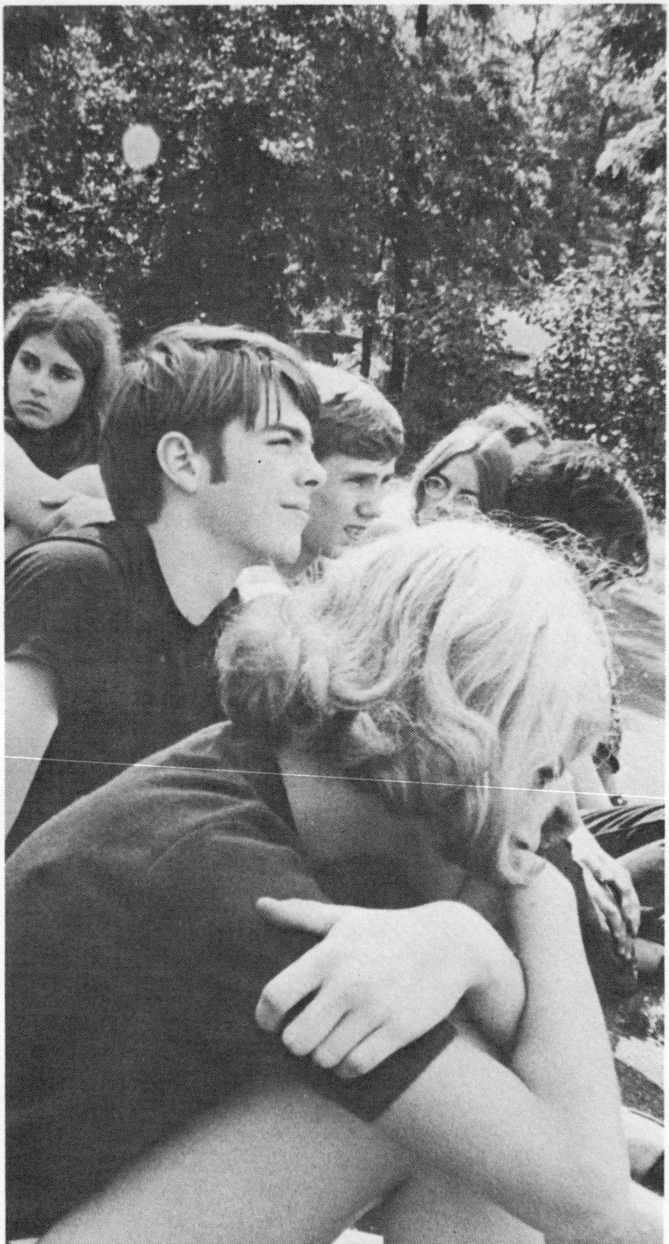

HAS THE CHURCH LOST OUR CHILDREN?

BY MARY REED NEWLAND

The trouble is that it used to be easy — to raise children who would stay in the Church. All you had to do was to be good Catholics and send them to Catholic school or religion class. To be sure, every so often someone's child grew up to become fallen-away, but that could usually be accounted for by one of several reasons (mixed marriage, non-Catholic college, radical friends, low life). And along with prayers for their return went the conviction that nowhere else was the same splendid revelation of God, the same peace of mind, the same security available. Hopefully they would discover it sooner or later and, even if at death's door, come home at last.

Keeping Up with Our Catholic Faith

Then came the horrendous experience of the last decade. Hoards of young people who had been raised precisely as they should have been by good Catholic parents have walked away from the Church. Two burning questions beg for answers: "Why?" and "How can we make sure that the next generation won't do the same thing?"

Why Did They Leave Us?

There are probably lots of answers to "Why?" It has much to do with cultural revolution, the effect of instant information via the media and, let's admit it, the myopia of much of the Catholic community with respect to what were supposed to be the marks of Catholic Christians. How were we identified? Unfortunately not usually by the splendor of what the Church taught or how it was witnessed, but by the Friday abstinence, arguments over birth control, the infallibility of the Pope, the confessional, and the size of our families. With respect to issues like racial injustice, war, peace, other such things, we presented a rather cautious appearance. I remember one diocese in which the priests were forbidden to march at Selma. So much for prophetic vision.

With respect to the radiant truths we professed — un-death, resurrection, eternal life — Catholics did not seem to communicate the kind of exuberance that such beliefs ought to effect; in fact, underneath it all, the difference between Catholics and other people did not seem to be so great after all. To a young generation raised to ask "Why?" and to learn by doing, the action certainly wasn't where the Church was — and their experience of the Church was always of the local church. They got their social awareness, not from the pulpit, but from classes in social studies in high school and discovered along with it that Catholics had no corner on humanity, indeed, that the often-scorned "mere humanists" could have taught the Catholics a thing or two about altruism.

So parents who now find themselves with their nice Catholic children out of the Church ought — with some exceptions, I suppose — to stop beating themselves and asking, "Where did we go wrong?" Most of them did all they were supposed to do (given their lights) and many did more — but even *their* children have, for the moment, vacated the family pew. No one seems to have foreseen all the elements which would come together to create a climate in which all these young would leave the Church, which brings us to the second burning question: "How will we raise the next generation so they will stay in?"

You Can't Make the Child Believe

First of all, we had better forget about strategies for keeping them in. These constrict one's adventure with God and, from the outside looking in, anxious maneuvering is more irritating than helpful. Even the current doctrinal belt-tightening, the determination to restate Catholic teaching, corner the young and get it into them, can guarantee nothing — which ought to be obvious when we remember that the young of the great exodus were taught that way. They are not the children of the new catechetics.

No one would deny that it is important to state what Catholics believe, but that alone won't work if it is not acted out in living color. Lest anyone think, "Ah, *there* is the new formula," it must be added that even with splendid witness to put flesh on the bones (or bones in the flesh?) of Catholic teaching, there are two elements in the mix which cannot be eliminated: freedom and chemistry. No one can *make* a child believe, or be good, and no one yet has been able to chart the infinite number of chemical combinations (for want of a better description) which account for how people tick.

We are faced with the scarey business of admitting that there is no cookie cutter for turning out good Catholic children who will keep the faith and stay in the Church. We must settle for the risky business of believing that Christ and his Church can be irresistible to them, given their own way and their own time. We can provide the experience of faith lived, we can nurture in them the climate of joy and hope, which ought to characterize the life of Christians, we can tell them

Keeping Up with Our Catholic Faith

what the Church teaches and celebrate it — but beyond that we must leave them free to make of it what they will. Many times, even with the saints, it took painful experience with life to help them rediscover the treasures that had been laid in their laps as children.

All that said, we can go back to the beginning and start with the family — the most important force of all in the teaching and forming of young Christians, especially by *living out* the faith before their eyes.

Love the Baby

The first step is loving the baby, which hardly seems like teaching religion — but it is. It is, in fact, the first experience of God, and without it, words about God won't work. Loving a baby communicates to him/her (him, for the sake of simplicity — no offense intended) his first value, the value of self. Children measure their worth by the way they are treated — but don't we all? If you have never been loved, you can hardly believe you are lovable; and if you can't believe that, you can't love yourself, so certainly not your neighbor as yourself. It starts at about three months.

Children have strong loyalties, and the people they imitate best, if at all, are those they love and trust. All neighborhood arguments are settled with, "My father said so," and comparisons are introduced with, "My mother does it this way." Children have faith because their parents have, and in the God their parents know.

A Sister tells of a small boy in her religion class whose parents, once staunchly Catholic, changed to a Fundamentalist Church in protest over renewal in their parish. The little boy still attends class as a concession to a Catholic grandmother, but he now contends Catholic teaching as vigorously as he once supported it, not for reasons of faith or enlightenment, but because his loyalties shifted along with those of his parents.

Parents give children the idea of God they hold themselves,

Has the Church Lost Our Children?

and to pass on to them a God who is an old man, a heavenly policeman, an eye in the sky, will not serve young people who grow up studying the infinite complexities of the universe. In his book *Your God Is Too Small*, J. B. Phillips tells of a questionnaire which asked students, "Could God understand radar?" Each answer came back "No." Such a God is not credible to young people who watch man in space, and they will leave that God behind.

Parents give their children their sense of the boundlessness of God, and also of his personal attributes. Is God just and merciful, compassionate and understanding? Indeed, but young children cannot cope with such abstractions except through their experience of them — and their experience is with their parents. Do we teach that God never blames, or counts as sin, what wrong one does by accident or mistake or out of ignorance? It is translated by the justice and mercy we show when milk is spilled at the table or dirt tracked on the floor. Do we say God forgives wrongs if we are sorry, that one can always start all over again being good? The gentle forgiveness of parents, their loving embrace, their encouragement to "do better next time" is the child's first experience with a forgiving God.

Mom and Dad Are Virtue Book

Parents are the book in which children read all the virtues whose names and definitions were once memorized out of catechisms, but the substance of which was always learned and imitated when experienced. For example, the sensitivity of parents who truly believe that every person is sacred is reflected in the way they drive in traffic, how they treat people in crowds, their attitudes towards people who serve them in stores, at the garage, in restaurants, laundromats, sporting events. Parents who are honorable in even the smallest actions even when no one is looking ("No, darling, we mustn't get ahead of that lady — she was here first. . . ."), who respect property, others' rights and feelings, are acting out what it means to love one's neighbor as one's self.

A family's fortitude in accepting trials and disappointments ("Oh, well, you can't win 'em all, honey. . . .") is soaked in

Keeping Up with Our Catholic Faith

by the young when they experience their Christian parents persevering with courage and honor in a world where things sometimes hurt and people are unkind.

remember once when my father was cruelly insulted by a man not half his stature, how clearly his dignity revealed him as the nobler of the two when he refused to return in kind. It was an eloquent lesson for me. His was not a weakness but a strength, I knew even then, although it was years before I recognized it as one of the Beatitudes.

My father, a non-Catholic, was instilling in me that part of Catholic tradition known in those days as "offering it up" — a phrase which seems to have been derogated some these past years but bears preserving and teaching. His kind of "offering up" was not a license to behave like a martyr but shorthand for letting the evil stop with you and for giving up the dubious comfort of seeing it ricochet off to hurt still another, and another, and another. Such an example of endurance could only nurture honesty and self-knowledge, strength and good humor, and the kind of charity which, Paul says, "does not hold a grudge."

Beware the Consumer Craze

Likewise, the Christian family has a very vital role in teaching its children what posture to assume toward a world of gritty realities like inflation, consumerism and social injustice.

Oddly enough, the very inflation about which families complain so much these days could be converted by them into a blessing in disguise. Parents could see it as a signal for them to sound the call for self-discipline and sacrifice at a time when affluence and technology have become, at once, friend and foe. Freedom from things is not a choice easily made, but in retrospect families could learn to be grateful forever for the hardships which teach it, a lesson which makes great sense according to the Gospels, if non-sense elsewhere.

But even the guiding parents can be caught in the consumer current. Almost without knowing it, family recreation can

Has the Church Lost Our Children?

become shopping. Even as parents fear the appetites induced in their children by television advertising and promotion, the same parents see that they too soon need what they did not need, want what they did not want. Ladies dash into supermarkets with little lists and come out with their carts piled high. Children stroll through the mall with their parents, titillated by displays, laved by music, enchanted by greenery, fountains, baby animals, dolphins, kiddyland trains, displays, scents, sights, until they are tingling with the desire to have, to get, to buy — exactly as planned.

What can the family which is trying to be Christian do to protect its children from rampant consumerism in a push-button world where chores no longer exist and leisure time is surrendered to the exploiters?

Reminding the "Haves" of the "Have Nots"

The family can remind itself constantly that most people in the world know more of poverty, hunger, nakedness, sickness and death than affluence, that even the most modest American families live in luxury compared to the rest. We are less than 10 per cent of the world and we use over 75 per cent of its goods, which is immoral. The way for parents and children to cultivate conscience and discernment with respect to self-indulgence is to be ruthless about remembering the facts. Armed with these, a family cannot go on endlessly buying gadgets and goodies to add, eventually, to the pile of nonusable trash.

There are many ways that a family can inform its members about the plight of migrant workers, the poor in America, Latin America, as well as the starving of India, the drought-ridden of Africa. Bulletin board displays with news items, posters, lists of "We don't needs's" and "They do need's," Lenten and other sacrifices can make present to our families the agony of our brothers. Such parental initiative could help the whole family cool its consumer fever.

Out of just such a rich life of faith and understanding comes prayer, and parents teach their own kind of prayer to children. If God is the ambiance in which their household lives and moves, then all life becomes prayer and they will truly pray always, sometimes using traditional resources — Scripture, formal prayers, special devotions, liturgy — other times using the inspiration of the moment with words spontaneously chosen, or just by being joyful, reflective, grateful, active or quiet. Children know. That is how they learn to do it.

But where is the *doctrine*, someone will say. The doctrine is precisely *there* — in all the above. It can be defined and studied, and when that is helpful, fine. But to think it can be taught profitably without the *experience* of it is a vain wish. The family's principle role is to act out the doctrine.

For example: It teaches the Incarnation by celebrating Christmas and with the story of Jesus, but more — by making his love and presence enfleshed in them, in their love and service of others. It teaches Resurrection by celebrating Easter, but more — by believing joyfully that we don't die and by acting that way, treating death as another dramatic change at the end of mortal life, in quality rather like birth, the dramatic change at its beginning. The family translates Jesus' teaching about the contradictions of Christian life by facing its many crises — deaths — and surviving them, and in so doing it becomes wiser, "more abundantly" alive and unafraid. It teaches the Gospel statement that Jesus is to be identified with every man by seeing him in every man — "Who comes to the door is Christ."

Young people who grow up in such a setting of faith and witness must, even so, be left free to choose. But they are free, whether we like it or not, and strangely enough when they exercise their freedom and wander off, they often are in search of what they have left behind. Why? Bad example? Not always; but even when it is, what they search for is the truth bad example has betrayed.

Much of the time a youth drifts off because he has become blind to the too-familiar. The Church, like parents, becomes invisible and must be discovered all over again. "Only the

Has the Church Lost Our Children?

mature man can judge the nobility of his father." That is true. Does that mean that parents who have tried to make their children's splendid Catholic heritage visible need not have bothered, ought to have waited until they were mature? Not at all. It has been put there, and it is not that easy to be rid of. And when at last their search begins, the treasure is ready to be rediscovered.

Questions for Discussion

1. What possible motives does the author give for young people leaving organized religion?

2. What positive values serve as the foundation of organized religion? What benefits have you received from belonging to a church?

3. In what way can a parent expand the vision of God he or she conveys to the children?

4. The Declaration on Religious Freedom is the only document from Vatican II addressed to the whole world. In this document the Council Fathers state:
> This Vatican Synod declares that the human person has a right to religious freedom. This freedom means that all men are to be immune from coercion on the part of individuals or of social groups and of any human power, in such wise that in matters religious no one is forced to act in a manner contrary to his own beliefs. Nor is anyone to be restrained from acting in accordance with his own beliefs, whether privately or publicly, whether alone or in association with others, within due limits (Declaration on Religious Freedom, 2).

Is the intent of this statement to include children? Discuss the role of parents in teaching their children Christian values and practices. Could this become coercion?

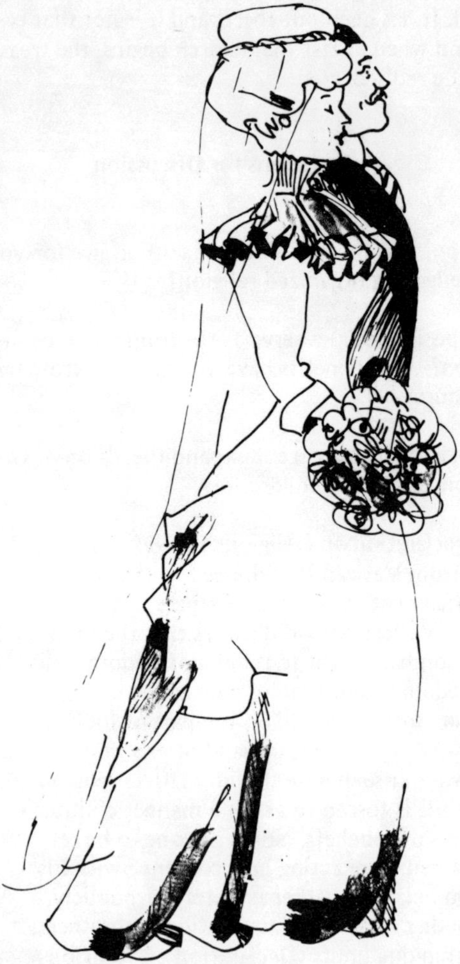

ARE CATHOLIC MARRIAGE LAWS CHANGING?

BY NORMAN PERRY, O.F.M.

Yes, no, and *maybe. Yes*—factually—*some* Church laws about marriage and its celebration are changing. *No,* there has been *no change in the most important things about marriage,* what is believed to be the very law of God himself. The Church still insists that a sacramental, consummated marriage cannot be broken except by death. And as for the *maybe*—well there is a great deal of *speculation* about what the Church possibly, can and might change.

What Has Changed

Most of the changes that have taken place involve marriages between Catholics and those of another or no faith. Formerly the law required a serious cause to dispense a Catholic from the canon law impediments prohibiting marriage to a non-Catholic Christian or someone not baptized. While still recognizing the difficulties of such marriages, the risk to the faith of the Catholic party, and urging against such marriages, the Holy See now allows bishops to dispense from these impediments for any just cause. An example of such a just cause would be the couple's love for each other and desire to enter a good marriage.

The present regulations do insist on the responsibility of the Catholic to safeguard his faith and, as far as possible, see that his children are baptized and formed in the faith. Accordingly the Catholic party must declare that he is ready to remove the dangers of falling away from the faith and promise to do all in his power to have all the children of the union baptized and brought up in the Catholic Church. But to provide for the conscience of the non-Catholic party, the laws no longer require similar promises on his part. It is recognized that at times it may be impossible for the Catholic to carry out his intention to have his children baptized and reared Catholic. The law does not demand the impossible. But the non-Catholic must be informed of the promises the Catholic is making. Both parties are to be instructed about the unity and permanence of marriage.

In any and every case Catholics are still bound by the form of marriage. In other words, marriage must take place before an authorized priest or deacon and two witnesses. Yet it is now possible for the bishop to dispense from this for a serious reason like the following: the family of the non-Catholic have a strong attachment to their own Church; a "Catholic" wedding would produce family hostility; or the non-Catholic has a relative who is a minister or rabbi.

If the wedding takes place in a Catholic church, the non-Catholic's clergyman may be invited to participate in the ceremony. He may read prayers, ask a blessing on the marriage and speak some words of congratulations or exhortation. When the marriage is celebrated in the Church of the non-Catholic, the ceremonies of that Church are used. In

Are Catholic Marriage Laws Changing?

such weddings the non-Catholic clergyman is the witness to the vows and exchange of consent of the bridal couple. The bishop may also allow a priest to be present and offer prayers and congratulations. In no case may there be two ceremonies or two different celebrations of the marriage rites—even on the same occasion, one after another.

In 1966 the excommunication of Catholics marrying before a non-Catholic minister was abolished, both for the future and the past. This means that those who marry before a non-Catholic minister without the bishop's permission are not excommunicated even though they sin by violating the Church's law and may not receive Holy Communion. Those who in years gone by broke this law are no longer excommunicated even though they must still confess this past act and validate the marriage before receiving the Eucharist. The chief effect is to make the way back to the sacraments a little easier and less complicated when this law has been violated.

Liturgical Changes

There is no intention to linger here over liturgical changes, as important as they are. Many variations of the ceremony are possible according to preferences of individual couples. There is a rich variety of readings and prayers from which to choose. The parents of the bride and the groom may lead them to the altar. Brothers and sisters, cousins, or uncles and aunts may read some of the scriptural lessons and present the gifts. Bride and groom may carry the sign of peace to their families.

Changes at the Marriage Court

Among the most important changes taking place are those in the Church marriage courts. Not only are the courts dealing more quickly and effectively with the cases they try, but they are recognizing new reasons to declare marriages invalid or null (i.e., that there never really was a marriage). In many cases the Holy See permits the use of one judge instead of three to decide whether a marriage is valid or not. Persons may have their cases tried in the place they live rather than the diocese where the marriage took place. Some marriage tribunals have increased their efficiency by using tape recorders and the telephone to gather testimony. The Brooklyn diocese plays such tapes for medical experts and psychiatrists, who can then give an oral and recorded opinion on the past emotional or psychic ability of a patient to contract a marriage. Weeks and months of gathering evidence and testimony are shortened to days and hours.

Perhaps most important is the recent recognition by tribunal officials and the Roman Rota that psychic impotence as well as physical impotence can render marriage impossible. The Roman Rota and diocesan marriage courts are accepting the testimony of psychiatrists that some persons are unable because of psychic inability to fulfill the marriage duties of procreating and educating children and accepting the responsibilities of marriage. Such persons, consequently, are considered incapable of obliging themselves to the marriage contract.

Teen Marriages

Along with the recognition that some people are never psychologically able to contract marriage has come the realization that maturity is always important to successful marriage. A dozen dioceses in the United States and Canada have made special rules for the marriages of teenagers. Those rules demand that teenagers receive special counseling before marriage. The counselor evaluates their readiness for marriage and the bishop, on the recommendation of the parish priest and the counselor, may ask the couple to postpone the marriage until they are better prepared or even, in extreme cases, refuse permission for the wedding to take place. Not only does the counselor help evaluate the readiness of the young couple for marriage but he also gives them positive assistance and guidance.

Speculations of the Theologians

Those who grew up in the Church before 1962 may feel that the law has changed tremendously. Catholics schooled in the

Are Catholic Marriage Laws Changing?

Vatican II decade may think that the changes have been minimal and the least that could have been done to meet the demands of ecumenism and the late 20th century. Both groups ought to know that the marriage laws are under further study and consideration. The general revision of the whole code of canon law will probably bring other changes. It is too early to tell whether those changes will be largely technical and procedural or of substantial importance.

Whatever changes are still to come will be influenced by the Church's reaction to the speculations of present-day theologians and the suggestions of canonists. The magisterium (Pope and bishops) will either affirm what has been considered the traditional understanding of Christian marriage and confirm present laws or act according to what they believe are new and deeper insights into God's law.

Because much of the speculation going on concerns the possibility or impossibility of divorce and remarriage, it is important to know that the Vatican Doctrinal Congregation has reminded the bishops that those who are invalidly married may not receive the Sacrament of Penance or Communion unless they are living as "brother and sister." Cardinal Seper, prefect of the congregation, warned the bishops to be on guard against "new opinions which deny or seek to cast doubt on the doctrine of the indissolubility of marriage."

Cardinal Seper and the congregation have reaffirmed the belief of the Church that a sacramental consummated marriage cannot be dissolved. They are telling us again that if your Catholic Aunt Jane married a baptized man and had sexual intercourse with him, that marriage cannot be dissolved or nullified. She cannot obtain a civil divorce, remarry and receive the sacraments. The bishops were told to exercise great care so that all those who teach religion and are officials in the Church tribunals remain faithful to the teaching of the Church in all that regards the indissolubility of marriage.

Keeping Up with Our Catholic Faith

Suggested Legal Reforms

Father Bernard Häring has proposed what sounds like a very simple change in the present law. Today's canon law requires that whenever there is doubt about validity, the marriage bond is to be given the benefit of the doubt. In other words, if a marriage is doubtfully valid, the parties may not remarry. Father Häring suggests that this should be reversed. He proposes that when a doubtfully valid marriage cannot be saved, the couple should be free to enter a new valid marriage. This change may sound simple but it would affect the lives of many people.

Another simple-sounding, but far-reaching, change is proposed for the discussion of canonists and theologians by Father Paul Palmer, professor of sacramental theology at St. John's Provincial Seminary in Plymouth, Michigan. He suggests that the Church extend the words of St. Paul about those married to unbelievers (the Pauline Privilege) to those married to *baptized* unbelievers. Father Palmer argues that Christian marriage is a *graced covenant* between two baptized *believers* and that only such a Christian marriage when consummated is wholly indissoluble. Many who have been baptized, says Father Palmer, do not really enter marriage as believers. He theorizes it would be according to the mind of St. Paul that upon the conversion of such a person the Church free him to enter a really Christian marriage.

Speaking as a sociologist, Father Andrew Greeley suggests Church marriage legislation came into being when marriage was viewed primarily as a contract concerned basically with the transmission of inheritance and property. Father Greeley says that today, when marriage is considered more an interpersonal commitment, the Church's matrimonial apparatus is irrelevant. Father Greeley wonders aloud if the Church shouldn't stop making marriage laws and maintaining marriage courts. He believes the Church might spend its effort better in preaching the religious ideals of marriage and helping couples to live such ideals. Some who agree that the Church should drop the marriage courts would place the responsibility for deciding any questions about the morality of a particular marriage in the conscience of the individual and the confessional.

Speculation About the Bond of Marriage

Certainly the most startling theorizing going on concerns the bond of marriage itself and its unbreakable character. Theologians of some stature are advocating a serious restudy of what Jesus actually meant when he said, as St. Matthew (5:31-32) quotes him, "What I say to you is: everyone who divorces his wife—lewd conduct is a separate case—forces her to commit adultery. The man who marries a divorced woman likewise commits adultery." Various understandings and interpretations are proposed. Some argue that these words of Jesus fall within the Sermon on the Mount and should be taken as the statement of an *ideal* rather than a law.

Others propose that St. Paul's words (I Cor. 7:10-16) explaining the Christian teaching about marriage and allowing a Christian to separate from a non-Christian who refuses to live in peace, should not be restricted to nonsacramental marriages. Thomas Thompson in the *Journal of Ecumenical Studies, 1969* insists that Jesus condemned divorce in all marriages. If St. Paul and the Church could permit Christians to divorce hostile non-Christians and remarry, Thompson says, the Church can decide that even in some sacramental marriages a married life of peace is not possible and allow a new marriage to take place.

At the same time, moral and pastoral theologians are concerned with the plight of Catholics who have been divorced and entered new marriages without being able to prove their first marriages were invalid. Some moralists, groping for a way to help them return to the sacraments, suggest the possibility of a "death of marriage." They propose that a marriage at one time Christian, a marriage "in the Lord," may have "died" and can in no way be brought back to life.

These writers believe the Church should examine the possi-

Keeping Up with Our Catholic Faith

bility of declaring such marriages dead, the bond destroyed, and the partners free to enter a new marriage that will be truly Christian. In other cases they propose that confessors should admit to the sacraments men and women who are convinced in conscience that they were never validly married but cannot prove it in a Church tribunal. In such cases every effort would be made to avoid scandal (misleading others). Some dioceses had actually established a public procedure to deal with such cases before being instructed by the Holy See to discontinue it. [We repeat here that readers must remember the most recent instruction of the Doctrinal

What Has Changed

A *just* rather than a serious cause necessary for a dispensation to enter a mixed marriage.

Bishops are able to dispense from the Catholic form for marriage if there is a serious reason. Thus possible to have a non-Catholic minister officiate.

No promise required of non-Catholic party to a mixed marriage.

Nuptial Mass permitted if non-Catholic party to a mixed marriage is baptized.

Excommunication (future and past) removed for marriage before a non-Catholic minister, agreement to have child baptized by non-Catholic minister or educated in non-Catholic religion.

Procedural rules for handling marriage cases in diocesan tribunals.

Special procedures have been added in some dioceses for teenage marriages.

Are Catholic Marriage Laws Changing?

Congregation that those who are invalidly married may not receive the sacraments.]

Conclusions

What conclusions should the ordinary Catholic draw from the changes and speculation taking place? First, we should realize that speculation is only speculation. It opens up avenues of thought, ideas to explore and test out. It is not the basis for action until it has been proved and verified. Contrary to much that is being said is the centuries-old

What Hasn't Changed

Dispensation still needed for mixed marriage.

Catholic party to mixed marriage still has obligation and must promise "to do all in his power" to have children baptized and brought up in Catholic faith.

Form of marriage. Must take place before pastor of place or his delegate and two witnesses.

All canonical impediments remain.

Marriage for life.

Marriage between one man and one woman.

Sacramental, consummated marriage cannot be dissolved.

Marriage is for the procreation of children.

Areas of Speculation

When is a marriage truly consummated?

Just what is the power of the Church to dissolve marriages? Can, and when can, the Church permit a new marriage, as in the case of the Pauline Privilege or the Privilege of Faith?

What makes a person unable or incapable to contract a real marriage?

What is the exact meaning or force of Christ's words on marriage, "Everyone who divorces his wife—lewd conduct is a separate case—forces her to commit adultery. The man who marries a divorced woman likewise commits adultery" (Matthew 5:32)?

Keeping Up with Our Catholic Faith

understanding and practice of the Church. Dr. John T. Noonan, Jr., has shown in *The Power to Dissolve* that in Church history a fully consummated marriage contracted "in the Lord" and intended to be lived out as a sacrament is absolutely indissoluble in the absence of evidence to the contrary. Reexamination and restudy do not necessarily mean change. They often result in proving the present practice correct and show the faults in new arguments and theories.

Second, the disciplinary law of the Church is subject to change. The future and a new code of canon law can be expected to bring changes in the present laws. Every revision of canon law has done this. And if changes and development take place, they should be accepted as the Church's best understanding of what is just and good for the spiritual welfare of her members. If some are helped back to the sacraments by changes, we should rejoice with them rather than resent change.

And if with possible changes we realize that Catholics living and marrying today will be free of burdens or prohibitions that troubled and bound our parents or brothers and sisters in the past, we should not be angry and bitter because of the freedom of the new or the suffering of the past. This was the fault of the elder brother in the prodigal son story who resented the mercy that his returning brother received. We should be genuinely glad of new insights that may ease the burdens of those around us. We should realize that laws are made with the understanding of those who make them to fit the problems and demands of their time. Laws are constantly being updated and changed in accord with new needs, new understandings and new times. We do not become angry because men, who would have died 10 or 20 years ago, are saved today by kidney machines, organ transplants, chemotherapy and antibiotics. We do not get angry because our children have schooling and advantages that were denied us. A less burdensome law, if it develops, should not cause anger or dismay in today's Catholic.

Are Catholic Marriage Laws Changing?

Questions for Discussion

1. What change of *attitude* is reflected in the new laws concerning marriages between Catholics and non-Catholic Christians or persons not baptized?

2. What new ground for the annulment of a marriage is now being recognized by the Church marriage courts? Why?

3. Has the Church, at this point, changed her understanding of the permanence of a validly entered and consummated sacramental marriage?

4. Father Greeley feels that the view of marriage prevalent when the present canon law was written is not the view of marriage in our time. What is the current understanding of marriage around which he believes new legislation should be formulated?

5. If, in the future, the law of the Church is changed to allow some divorced Catholics to remarry and receive the sacraments, how would you respond to a person who said, "Anything goes now—there's no point to being faithful to your wife if you can get married again."